EIR (ISSN 0273-6314) *is published weekly
(50 issues), by EIR News Service, Inc.,
P.O. Box 17390, Washington, D.C. 20041-0390.
(703) 297-8434*

European Headquarters: E.I.R. GmbH, Postfach
Bahnstrasse 9a, D-65205, Wiesbaden, Germany
Tel: 49-611-73650
Homepage: http://www.eir.de
e-mail: info@eir.de
Director: Georg Neudecker

Montreal, Canada: 514-461-1557
eir@eircanada.ca

Denmark: EIR - Danmark, Sankt Knuds Vej 11,
basement left, DK-1903 Frederiksberg, Denmark.
Tel.: +45 35 43 60 40, Fax: +45 35 43 87 57. e-mail:
eirdk@hotmail.com.

Mexico City: EIR, Sor Juana Inés de la Cruz 242-2
Col. Agricultura C.P. 11360
Delegación M. Hidalgo, México D.F.
Tel. (5525) 5318-2301
eirmexico@gmail.com

President Trump Moves To Crush British Coup

President Trump Orders Key 'Russiagate' Documents Declassified As Putin Outflanks War Party in Syria

by Barbara Boyd

Sept. 18—Late afternoon on Monday, Sept. 17, the White House Office of the Press Secretary issued the following statement from the Press Secretary, which we include here in its entirety:

STATEMENT FROM THE PRESS SECRETARY

Issued on: September 17, 2018

At the request of a number of committees of Congress, and for reasons of transparency, the President has directed the Office of the Director of National Intelligence and the Department of Justice (including the FBI) to provide for the immediate declassification of the following materials: (1) pages 10-12 and 17-34 of the June 2017 application to the FISA court in the matter of Carter W. Page; (2) all FBI reports of interviews with Bruce G. Ohr prepared in connection with the Russia investigation; and (3) all FBI reports of interviews prepared in connection with all Carter Page FISA applications.

In addition, President Donald J. Trump has directed the Department of Justice (including the FBI) to publicly release all text messages relating to the Russia investigation, without redaction, of James Comey, Andrew McCabe, Peter Strzok, Lisa Page, and Bruce Ohr.

According to press accounts on Monday evening, the documents will be released "expeditiously" with the FISA application coming first, together with the FBI interview reports of Bruce Ohr and Carter Page. It is anticipated that the text messages will take a longer time to release. This dramatic action by the President occurs at the same time as a grand jury in the District of Columbia considers criminal indictments of key officials for leaks of classified information generated in the Russiagate investigation to the news media, according to widespread press reports.

By all accounts, the declassification of these documents will allow the public to grasp, for the first time, a clear view of the most frightening political abuse of power in American history. The Obama Administration, acting at the behest of the British government, set out to destroy Donald Trump's candidacy on behalf of his opponent Hillary Clinton, using the full national security and law enforcement powers of the United States to do so and then to destroy his Presidency.

British intelligence, through MI6's Christopher Steele, produced a political hit piece on Donald Trump, which was paid for by Hillary Clinton. Steele's dirty dossier asserted that Trump had nefarious connections to Russia and that Putin had compromised him. On four separate occasions, Obama Justice Department officials went to the top-secret FISA court, established under the Foreign Intelligence Surveillance Act of 1978, to obtain complete surveillance of Trump campaign volunteer Carter Page, and through him on the Trump campaign itself. According to Steele's deliberately false claim, Carter Page was a central figure in the Trump/Moscow nexus.

The same Justice Department officials knew, when they made the application, that Steele's dossier was false concerning Page. They never informed the court that Steele's information had been paid for by Hillary Clinton, Trump's opponent, and that it had never been verified as required by FISA procedures. Steele's dirty dossier was used by John Brennan's CIA as the pretext for entrapment operations against Trump campaign volunteers George Papadopoulos and Carter Page, conducted, for the most part, on British soil. All the while, the FBI and others were leaking endlessly to the news media that there was a serious FBI investigation of candidate Trump which implicitly involved charges amounting to treason with respect to Russia. James Comey, Andrew McCabe, Peter Strzok, Lisa Page, and Bruce Ohr were key players in this orchestrated information warfare and political espionage operation against Donald Trump.

LaRouche PAC has repeatedly called for the President to declassify, in addition to these documents, all British-spawned documents demanding investigation of Donald Trump and his campaign associates, so that the American people can understand that this operation had profound strategic implications. It was, and is, nothing less than an attempt to take out President Trump because he sought an end to the perpetual wars supporting the Anglo-Dutch monetary system, and sought rational relationships with both Russia and China in the context of rebuilding the physical economy of the United States.

In addition, LaRouche PAC has asked the President to declassify all the documents concerning the 9/11/2001 attack on the United States by the British Saudi asset, particularly focusing on Robert Mueller's role, as FBI Director, in obstructing and covering up any investigation of the Saudi role in the attack. Mueller, the Special Counsel, should be exposed as the architect of the 9/11 coverup concerning the murder of nearly three thousand Americans, and also as a key architect of the unconstitutional surveillance state which was built following 9/11. This declassification will deal the most fateful blow to the ongoing coup.

On the Syrian front, after a meeting in Sochi on security in Syria, between Russian President Vladimir Putin and Turkish President Recep Tayyip Erdogan, Russia announced that there will be no general assault on Idlib, at present, against the terrorists, but rather a collaboration between the governments of Syria, Russia, and Turkey to isolate and move against the jihadis there, while protecting the civilian population as much as possible.

This strikes a significant blow against the British-led mobilization for war in Syria. The war party has claimed that any Syrian government assault on Idlib terrorists—who are members of al Qaeda and its offshoots—would be grounds for the United States, UK, and France to launch strikes against Syria, possibly provoking an all-out war. Putin has thus outflanked the warhawks. Though not routing them, he has exposed them. What remains to be seen on this front, however, is whether the British forces can successfully pull off a false-flag gas attack on civilians in Syria and blame it on the Assad government, precipitating military retaliation. Such a false-flag attack has been in preparation for weeks and the preparations for it have been observed and documented by the Russian government in warnings to the international community.

EIR Contents

www.larouchepub.com Volume 45, Number 38, September 21, 2018

White House/Shealah Craighead

Cover This Week: President Donald Trump welcomes guests to the Congressional Medal of Honor Society reception, Sept. 12, 2018, in the East Room of the White House.

PRESIDENT TRUMP MOVES TO CRUSH BRITISH COUP

I. A Four-Power Agreement for a New Paradigm

II. LaRouche's Ideas in Asia

III. The Education of Lyndon LaRouche

Can Beauty Silence the Drums of War?

by John Sigerson

Sigerson is the co-author of A Manual on the Rudiments of Tuning and Registration, *and is the Musical Director and co-conductor of the Schiller Institute NYC chorus. He is an accomplished tenor and plays piano and string bass.*

Sept. 15—Among a number of public events marking the 17th anniversary of the al-Qaeda attacks on New York and Washington, one stood out as not merely a memorialization of past horrors, but as a herald of a future in which true justice shall be served, not only for those who died on that day and who continue to die of its after-effects, but also for a humiliated nation and an aching world.

It was a concert of Classical music and poetry, held at St. Anthony of Padua Church, in lower Manhattan, a church which served as a sanctuary on that day of infamy 17 years ago. Organized and sponsored by the Schiller Institute NYC Chorus, with the support of the Schiller Institute founded by Helga Zepp-LaRouche, it was the necessary counterpoint to the Schiller Institute's conference held two days later, as reported on elsewhere in this issue.

No less a personage than Gen. Douglas MacArthur knew well that such expressions of Man's most sublime cultural achievements are the surest way to avert the destruction of the human species through war, by changing not *what* men think, but *how* they think, how they judge. As MacArthur stated at the conclusion of World War II:

Schiller Institute

The Schiller Institute NYC Chorus, singing at the 9/11 memorial concert at St. Anthony of Padua Church, in lower Manhattan, September 11, 2018.

The problem basically is theological and involves a spiritual recrudescence and improvement of human character that will synchronize with our almost matchless advances in science, art, literature and all material and cultural developments of the past two thousand years. It must be of the spirit if we are to save the flesh.

Upon entering the beautiful church, the audience heard a single solo violin, played masterfully by Gabrielle Fink, sounding two movements of Johann Sebastian Bach's Solo Sonata No. 1 in G minor, a work replete with the same kind of ironical juxtapositions with which any thinking person is confronted in grappling with today's very real question of whether the United States might once again be manipulated into violating the principles on which the republic was founded.

Schiller Institute spokesman Dennis Speed made this explicit in his opening remarks from the pulpit:

We are gathered here not to commemorate tragedy, but to avert it. Even as we gather here tonight, as was true 17 years ago, the drums of war are being beaten by a group of people in the world spanning various nations and agencies, who seek to induce the United States into an attack on Syria—a Syria which, together with Russia, and also with the assistance of the United States, has significantly reduced and cornered those forces, sometimes called al-Nusra, sometimes called al-Qaeda, but always appropriately called evil, which were part of the carrying out of the attacks here 17 years ago—attacks for which this church, and several other venues in this neighborhood, served as sanctuary—as makeshift hospitals, and, in some cases, as the place where last rites were given.

And that is our situation tonight. It's important to *say* that, because we are led to believe, in our world, that tragedy is a necessity. It is not.

Referencing Virginia State Senator Richard Black's interview following his recent fact-finding trip to Syria, Speed praised Senator Black's courageous commitment to preventing the United States from carrying out, once again, a blind, wrong intervention. "And in this case, the irony would be that such an intervention would constitute the United States acting as the air force for the very al Nusra and al-Qaeda forces that participated in the 9/11 attack."

Speed pointed to the real solution to such blindness:

When we bring people together, and we use *music* to go beyond the mundane, the banal, the literal, the didactic, the ideological, then the better angels of our nature become poised and armed to overthrow even our own desire for ignorance and blindness.

As one man once said, there are no real mysteries, there's only blindness. And blindness can always be overcome by Truth. But to fortify people of goodwill who perhaps have lost their way, sometimes that Truth must be sung, not said. And we hope that tonight, as we stand here in honor of those dead at the bottom of the World Trade Center, and those who have died since because of diseases and because of their valiant work that day, we hope that what we do here tonight to renew our commitment, and the commitment of the United States itself, to the ideal of Freedom, may proceed through Beauty, not war.

The Music

There followed a well-crafted succession of musical works, performed by four vocal soloists—soprano Indira Mahajan, alto Linda Childs, tenor Everett Suttle, and bass Paul An—accompanied by Robert Wilson on piano, along with the Schiller Institute NYC Chorus directed by John Sigerson and Diane Sare and accompanied by Yuting Zhou on piano.

Since a video of the concert is available on the Schiller Institute's website, I will focus here on just a few highlights.

Early in the program was a performance of a very special, brief unaccompanied choral work by Johannes Brahms, with lyrics taken from the funeral scene of Friedrich Schiller's allegorical poem "The Song of the Bell," juxtaposing the farmer's sowing of seed, to the coffins bearing the deceased: "far more precious seed," which, we hope, "shall blossom to a more beautiful destiny."

Brahms composed the piece as a funeral tribute to his mentor and dear friend, the composer Robert

Schumann; but it is also a tribute to Brahms's hero Ludwig van Beethoven, in that the opening four notes, sung in unison, are identical to the opening four notes played by the soloist in Beethoven's Opus 69 Sonata for Piano and Violoncello.

To set the tone for Brahms's all-too-brief setting, Schiller Institute President William F. Wertz, Jr. recited a devastating section of Schiller's poem leading up to Brahms's lyrics, in a translation by his late wife Marianna Wertz.

Each vocal soloist paired a Negro Spiritual arranged by such composers as Harry Burleigh and Roland Hayes, with a German *Lied* composed by Franz Schubert, all accompanied by Robert Wilson. A listing of each masterly rendition cannot possibly convey the depth and profundity of their performances. Therefore, I point out only two.

The first was Wilson's own arrangement of the Spiritual, "Deep River," sung by alto Linda Childs, a setting which includes new motivic elements not present in other arrangements of this piece. As Wilson explained afterwards, he encountered this new material in an unpublished setting by John Rosamond Johnson, who is perhaps most famous for composing "Lift Every Voice and Sing" to a poem by his brother James Weldon Johnson. This juxtaposition of additional material, seemingly unrelated but in fact united in a higher dimension, is the hallmark of great Classical composition.

No less moving was Wilson's accompaniment to Linda Childs' singing of Schubert's "Litanei," a poem in the form of a prayer for All Souls' Day, with each stanza ending with, "May all souls rest in Peace!" Instead of just "playing the notes" in Schubert's score, Wilson reached "behind the notes" (to use a concept emphasized by Wilhelm Furtwängler), subtly enhancing the accompaniment. As Wilson commented following the concert, "When I play that piece, I hear instruments," and indeed under his hands, the postlude of each stanza grew into what one could easily mistake as a full orchestra, but as if Schubert himself had been at the keyboard.

Interspersed were performances of Spirituals by the 85-strong Schiller Institute NYC Chorus, directed by Diane Sare. As a testament to the growing reputation of this unique institution, NBC-TV featured the chorus in advance of the performance, reporting that the Chorus had "been given the honor" of memorializing 9/11 in downtown Manhattan—which is inaccurate, since in fact the Schiller Institute NYC Chorus *seized* that honor, because so few other institutions had planned concert events around the city! Both NBC and ABC filmed parts of the concert itself and included it in their day's coverage—quite uncharacteristically, and in violation of the general "orders" handed down to the mainstream media, never to so much as mention Lyndon LaRouche or LaRouche-inspired efforts.

Concluding the concert was the "Lamb of God" section of Beethoven's sublime *Mass in C Major*, Opus 86, directed by John Sigerson. As Beethoven makes even more evident in his later grand *Missa Solemnis*, the image of the Lamb of God, in danger of being slaughtered in senseless warfare, is clearly contrasted with the concluding, gently but firmly victorious "Dona nobis pacem" (Grant us peace), celebrating humanity's recovery from the infantile social disease of "geopolitics," and its embracing of a new paradigm of relations among men and nations.

The Schiller Institute NYC Chorus will perform the entire work, along with Beethoven's *Choral Fantasia* Opus 80, this coming Nov. 18 at St. Bartholomew's Church in New York.

Mere applause at the end of such a concert, with such an intent, would have been misplaced: Instead, the audience was invited to join with the chorus in singing the three-part traditional canon "Dona nobis pacem." And sing they did, followed by an almost eerie silence, in expectation of some future goodness, unspoken, yet strongly felt.

Schiller Institute Conference

Toward a Four Power Agreement for a New Paradigm of Development

Thursday, September 13, 2018
New York City

Musical Prelude

"Auf der Donau," by Franz Schubert. Paul An, bass;
Robert Wilson, piano
"Partita in D minor" (BWV 1004) and Sarabande, by
J.S. Bach. Gary Ianco, violin

Greetings

Liliana Gorini, Chairwoman of MoviSol, LaRouche's
movement in Italy. "Italy and China Cooperate to
Develop Africa"
Ulf Sandmark, leader of the LaRouche movement in
Sweden. "Every Step of Syrian Reconstruction Is a
Celebration of the New Silk Road"
Ramasimong Phillip Tskolibane, leader of the
LaRouche movement in South Africa. "The
United States Must Help Save Africa"

Panel I
The End of Colonialism:
A New Shared Future for Humanity

KEYNOTE
Helga Zepp-LaRouche
Founder of the Schiller Institutes
"The End of Colonialism: A New Shared
Future for Humanity"

Jason Ross
Schiller Institute science advisor
"Expanding 'Possibility' "
Speech not available at press time.

Panel II
Only a Four Power Agreement Can Prevent War, Assure Development

Xu Wenhong, PhD
Deputy Secretary-General, Center for Belt and Road
Studies, Chinese Academy of Social Sciences, Beijing
"The Belt and Road: World Cooperation
for the Benefit of All"

Richard Black
Virginia State Senator
"Reconciliation and Rebuilding in Syria,
as a Great Battle Looms in Idlib"

James George Jatras
Former U.S. diplomat and former advisor to
the Republican Party leadership
"It's Time for All of Us to Escape the 'Trans-
Atlanticism' Straitjacket"

Dmitry Polyanskiy
First Deputy Permanent Representative, Russian Federation
Permanent Mission to the United Nations
"We are Keen for Friendship and Economic
Partnership, No Matter How Difficult It May Seem"

Roger Stone
Political consultant, lobbyist and strategist
"It's a Fight for the Republic,
Not the Two-Party Duopoly"

The End of Colonialism: A New Shared Future for Humanity

HELGA ZEPP-LAROUCHE'S KEYNOTE

The End of Colonialism: A New Shared Future for Humanity

This is the edited transcript of Helga Zepp-LaRouche's keynote speech to the Schiller Institute's conference in New York, September 13, 2018.

Thank you. Ladies and gentlemen, dear friends of the Schiller Institute: We need to be conscious of the historical moment in which we find ourselves. I don't think I'm exaggerating when I say that from the standpoint of what Friedrich Schiller would call Universal History, we have arrived at what he calls in his dramas, a *punctum saliens*. What he means by that is that the development of the entirety of universal history in the drama comes to a point where all the options up to that point are exhausted. It's a dramatic moment where everything depends entirely on the moral character of the main actor or the main figure on stage, if the drama will be a tragedy or if it has the potential to lead to a better outcome.

From the standpoint of universal history, if you take the entire, many millions of years, but especially the last 10,000 to 20,000 years, the last 100 years, I think we are reaching such a point in history, where, as my husband Lyndon LaRouche has said many times, the outcome of this historical period is entirely due to the moral character of the people. The question is posed: Does mankind have the moral fitness to survive or not?

Certain leading forces are now in a position to implement solutions, because the solutions to the crisis

Schiller Institute

Helga Zepp-LaRouche, founder of the Schiller Institutes, and President of the German Schiller Institute.

exist. But will the people of America, the people of Europe, the people of other continents support these leaders to implement, do so?

Panorama of Current History

Let me give you a panoramic view. This will be different than what you would get from the mainstream media in the United States or Western Europe, for that matter. We now have an unprecedented coincidence of existential crises. You have, as Dennis just mentioned, the immediate danger of an escalation of crisis and confrontation with Russia. There have been warnings in the last weeks, put out by the Russian government, that they have evidence that a third false-flag chemical attack is being prepared in Syria.

They have film footage of the White Helmets and other terrorists bringing poison gas—sarin and other chemical weapons—and crews of the White Helmets are in place ready to film such a massacre. American TV crews have moved into the region of Idlib. This is all unfolding as the Syrians—with support of the Russian air force—are determined to take out the last concentration of terrorists in Syria, the successors of al-Qaeda, al-Nusra, and ISIS, all gathered in Idlib. The Syrian government is making use of its sovereign right to reconquer that last province of Syria, and the Russians are helping with the air support.

So, the idea is basically to have this false-flag chemical attack, have film crews film it, and then broadcast it

Proof the White Helmets 'Staged' a Chemical Attack in Syria?

Images purportedly proving that the White Helmets staged a chemical attack in Syria are actually stills from a movie set.

around the world. This operation is supported by a British mercenary organization called Olive; they are orchestrating this operation, sitting with 5,000 mercenaries in Abu Dhabi. Various forces in the United States, the British government, and the French have already declared that they are ready to act with a military strike the moment such so-called proof of a chemical attack "by the Assad government" is presented.

The German Defense Ministry has already developed contingency plans for German participation, and this time it won't be just air reconnaissance, but the use of Tornadoes to bomb military installations. And the research service of the German Parliament has just put out an expert opinion saying this is a complete violation of international law, because there is no UN Security Council decision, and it's a complete violation of the German *Grundgesetz* [Constitution], which forbids a war of aggression—in the light of German history, a very noteworthy clause. So, if Germany were to engage militarily by bombing Syria, it would be the first time since the Second World War that Germany would take the risk of a direct military confrontation with Russia.

President Trump is under permanent bombardment by people who are trying to carry out a coup against him—to impeach him and get him out of office. Should they succeed in luring him into authorizing a full-fledged attack by the U.S. military, this conflict has the potential to go out of control. What happens if these U.S.-British-French—potentially German—military strikes hit some Russian targets in Syria? Would the Russians be content and not react? Well, right now there is a huge flotilla of the Russian Navy in the eastern Mediterranean. In addition to 36 Russian naval vessels, the British and U.S. navies are also engaged in exercises in the area. Instead of denouncing the British accusations against Syria—and against Russia in the Skripal affair—U.S. officials have shown their willingness to participate in those British accusations.

It is important to see the Skripal affair in this context. The British have not presented one iota of evidence that Russia was involved in the attempt on the life of Sergei Skripal and his daughter, or the other two individuals later on. The British and German governments just said they have full confidence in the British assessment that indeed it was two [Russian] GRU military intelligence agents; but they gave no evidence.

You have to look at the other pre-war scenario which is being orchestrated. I know I'm probably stepping on some people's toes when I say this, but Senator John McCain's funeral was celebrated and orchestrated as a Hollywood-style spectacular staged to show McCain as America's greatest hero and patriot and Trump not fit for the White House—at least according to the media. International audiences know McCain very well, because of his yearly appearances at the Munich Security Conference, where he behaved as one of the worst warmongers in his tirades against Russia, against China, and against other so-called "enemies."

Added to that is the latest Bob Woodward book portraying President Trump as unfit for the White House and totally incapable, which is providing the arguments for the Democrats to go for using the 25th Amendment against him. Then you have the "Anonymous" op-ed in the *New York Times*, saying there are moles in the administration who are trying to undo all the dangerous things Trump is trying to do. Even Obama had to come out and say, this mole has no democratic legitimacy, because whoever he or she is, that person was not elected and has no right to determine policy for the United States. On the other hand, some voices say it was persons associated with the *New York Times* who wrote the op-ed, which is, I think, the more likely assessment.

In the context of all these attacks on Trump, Obama

came back fully onstage in Chicago, saying, "Is it so difficult to denounce the Nazis?" referring to Trump not condemning the Charlottesville, Virginia incident of a year ago, totally leaving out of the picture that it was Obama's Administration that helped the Nazi coup in Kiev to bring the Nazis back into power in Ukraine. It was on the same day that the Speaker of the House of the Rada [the Ukrainian parliament], demanded direct democracy in Ukraine "in the tradition of Adolf Hitler." So much for Obama's attack on Nazis.

Vostok-2018 military maneuvers on the Tsugol training range, Trans-Baikal Territory, Russia, Sept. 13, 2018.

What you have right now—and when you come from the outside as I do, you see it more clearly—is the mainstream media in the United States gearing up a pre-war hysteria; preparing the population to believe that Vladimir Putin is a demon; that Xi Jinping is an autocratic dictator; and that Trump is not fit for office. The question you must ask yourself is, where is this supposed to lead? Are they putting all of this out just for fun and then they will just stop? Or is there some intention behind it?

Looking at the military situation in Syria, since President Putin intervened militarily in Syria in 2015, Syria and Russia have now gained complete control of the airspace in Syria. For the remaining terrorists in Idlib, either they capitulate and give themselves up, or they will be killed. Therefore, the situation is on a complete hair-trigger. Note that Trump has so far not initiated any war. He promised during the election campaign that he would try to improve relations with Russia, and he has gone out of his way to develop a personal friendship with President Xi Jinping—unlike the Bush and Obama Administrations, which started several wars.

It is also very clear that right now we are in a countdown, where there is not one iota of doubt that the faction of the British Empire that includes the British government, the Democrats, and the neo-cons in the Republican Party, are trying everything to prevent Trump from fulfilling his campaign promises. Especially after the historic summit in Helsinki, where Trump and Putin met—about which Trump even recently said that this was one of the best meetings he has ever had—all hell broke loose. It is absolutely clear that this faction does not want Trump to move on this policy.

All of these things I described—the Syria attack plan, the Skripal orchestration, the Woodward book, the *New York Times* op-ed—these are all atmospherics to try to get Trump out of office one way or the other.

So, we are really back at a situation where this faction is risking preventive nuclear war to occur. It's what Truman did to Hiroshima and Nagasaki in 1945, for which there was no military reason because the Japanese had already capitulated. Bombing of these two cities was just to establish the reign of nuclear terror for control of the postwar period. The difference between 1945 and 2018, is that the nuclear arsenals of the United States and Russia are big and powerful enough to annihilate the human species several times over.

On March 1 of this year, President Putin announced on that Russia had developed new weapons systems based on new physical principles. For example, a highly maneuverable Mach-20 hypersonic missile that is not ballistic; nuclear-powered cruise missiles; a nuclear-powered submarine which can go high speed. He also announced—and this has been verified by various military experts—that these new weapons of Russia's will undo the entire anti-ballistic missile system the United States has been building in the last year; about which Russia has said many times that they will not and cannot allow Phase III and IV to be built because it would completely destroy the strategic balance to the disadvantage of Russia. So, Russia has moved against that by developing these new weapons systems.

The Vostok-2018 military exercises, which started

on Tuesday, in the Far East of Russia, is the largest military exercise since 1981, since the Soviet Union. It involves 300,000 Russian troops, including 6,000 airborne troops; over 1,000 warplanes, helicopters, drones, 36,000 pieces of armor, 80 combat and support ships. It involves the North Sea Fleet in the Arctic. The exercise is meant to test the capability of Russia's military to move rapidly over long distances and coordinate between its different branches. New here, apart from the size of it, is that for the first time 3,200 Chinese troops, 900 Chinese combat vehicles, and 30 aircraft are involved, in this way demonstrating a full-fledged military alliance between China and Russia. Also participating are Mongolian troops.

It is clear that Russia and China are coordinating their weapons systems and their command structures. It is a very clear signal to the war party in the West as to what they will have to deal with, if they risk the provocation.

The German political figure, Willy Wimmer who was the Deputy Defense Secretary in Helmut's Kohl government and is still a member of the Christian Democratic Union party, in the last ten days issued several warnings that the only person standing between us and the next war, which would annihilate all of mankind, is Donald Trump. You may think whatever you want about Trump, but I think on that point, Wimmer is absolutely right. Because if the Democrats succeed in impeaching Trump following the midterm elections, I think we would very clearly see a convergence of the war party in that direction. We now have less than two months until November 6 midterm elections in the United States.

The situation in the United States is already extremely polarized. When you talk to people, they are either for Trump or against Trump, and you can't have a rational discussion as to why. If you ask an anti-Trump person "Why are you anti-Trump?" "He's a dictator." If you say, "But he wants to have peace with Russia." "Yeah, that's because he likes dictators"—namely Putin. All rationality has disappeared. The hysteria has reached a point of historic escalation. What did people say after the breakthrough of the Singapore meeting in which Trump very successfully put the question of solving the North Korea crisis on the track of a solution? "Trump likes dictators, and that's why he's doing these things with Kim Jong-un."

NATO Expansion: What Gorbachev Heard

Michail Gorbachev discussing German unification with Hans-Dietrich Genscher and Helmut Kohl in Russia, July 15, 1990. Photo: Bundesbildstelle / Presseund Informationsamt der Bundesregierung.

Declassified documents show security assurances against NATO expansion to Soviet leaders from Baker, Bush, Genscher, Kohl, Gates, Mitterrand, Thatcher, Hurd, Major, and Woerner

Slavic Studies Panel Addresses "Who Promised What to Whom on NATO Expansion?"

New Documents: NATO Was Not to Go East

What you have in the United States right now is a complete group-think; or rather, a group non-think. Because people are not thinking about the long-term universal history, but they are completely brainwashed by the media narratives. If you ask people, "Why is Putin a dictator? After all, he was three times democratically elected; he has 80% of his population backing him up. So, why is he a dictator?" You hear, "He annexed Crimea." Well, that is not exactly what happened. Just recently, declassified documents from the National Security Archives at the George Washington University were published, showing very clearly that the Soviet Union, and then Russia, in the period of 1989, 1990, 1991, was given absolute assurances that there was no intention to expand NATO eastward.

These documents make very clear, however, that there was a conscious effort to mislead the Soviet Union and Russia about the intention of NATO to do exactly that. Gorbachev at that point received assurances that NATO would not expand past East Germany. Therefore, Gorbachev agreed to the German unification. There were written memorandums to this effect, and there is a speech by former NATO General Secretary Manfred Wörner from the May 17, 1990 in Brussels, where he said, "It is absolutely the fact that we will not move the NATO army outside of German territory." This is giving the Soviet Union absolute security guarantees so that they can agree to the German unification.

There are quotes and documents that then Secretary of State [James] Baker wrote to Gorbachev on the February 9, 1990, and this is a famous quote: "NATO will not expand one inch eastward." That is why the Soviet Union dissolved, peacefully, without using tanks; they agreed to German unification. And that is why today, the Russians are extremely upset about the treason of the Germans; because they agreed peacefully to the German unification, and now the Germans are about to participate in such provocations against Russia, including military maneuvers where the Bundeswehr is now at the Russian border in the Baltic countries—something which anyone having a sense of what happened in the Second World War between Germany and Russia, should never tolerate happening again.

So, instead of not moving one inch eastward, you have a long history which started with little steps: of regime change, of color revolution, changing the governments of Eastern Europe. And then finally, the speech of Tony Blair in 1999 in Chicago, in which he declared officially the end of the Peace of Westphalia, replacing the respect for the UN Charter for sovereignty, with so-called "humanitarian interventions," followed by the "right to protect"—the idea that any country can intervene in any other around the world, you just have to orchestrate the necessary lies to justify such action, as it happened in the case of Iraq, Afghanistan, Syria, and Yemen, which is a similar case

This policy has cost millions of people's lives in the war-affected countries. President Trump has said many times that these wars have cost $7 trillion and that's why he wants to end them. They should not continue. The *Washington Post* nitpicked: "No, no, it was only $4 trillion or $6 trillion but not $7."

This is what is really at stake. Trump says he wants to establish an order of peace with Russia and China. The British forces are trying to prevent him. That's why the forces of the British Empire are out to get him. Because once Trump succeeds in establishing such relationships with Russia and China, it would end forever the British Empire's geopolitical manipulation of the world.

New Paradigm of the New Silk Road

OK, so this is one situation. But what most Americans have no idea of, because, how could you? The mainstream media has yet to mention, even once, that there is already a different world emerging, namely the new paradigm of the New Silk Road dynamic.

Since Xi Jinping announced the New Silk Road in Kazakhstan in 2013, five years have passed. During that time the most unbelievable transformation of Latin America, of Asia, of parts of Europe, of Africa, has taken place, where many of the countries—about 80-100, plus a number of large international organizations—are now working together with China in win-win cooperation. In those short five years, China has established major development corridors, connecting China and Europe, within Asia; many cargo trains full of goods are being exchanged; Africa is completely changing. Chinese investments over those five years have totaled $5 trillion.

What has developed is a completely new system of international relations, based on sovereignty, based on the respect for the other social system, noninterference, and more and more countries are joining in. Only last month, the BRICS nations—Brazil, Russia, India, China, and South Africa—joined with the Shanghai Cooperation Organization (SCO), and the Eurasian Economic Union (EAEU). At the July 25-27 BRICS Summit in Johannesburg, South Africa, saw the formation of something called the "Global South" which is practically the entirety of what used to be called the "Third World." It's the G77, it's Mercosur, it's the Organization of Islamic Cooperation, it's the African Union, and many regional organizations, all agreeing that they will build a new system of international relations.

At that summit, what Xi Jinping said is beautiful: "Science and technology, as the primary production forces, have provided inexhaustible power driving progress of human civilization." And he said that because Africa has the most developing countries, the African continent has the largest development potential of anybody. At the same summit, Vladimir Putin said that Russia will help to lift Africa up by bringing power to the 600 million people who still have no access to electricity, by not only providing gas and oil, but by helping the African countries to build up nuclear power for all of them.

The BRICS conference in South Africa last month and then this historic summit of the Forum on China-Africa Cooperation (FOCAC) at the beginning of September in Beijing—with 53 heads of state and government participating, mostly presidents, the rest being five prime ministers—I really think established the of-

The Beijing Summit of the Forum on China-Africa Cooperation opens in the Great Hall of the People, Beijing, China, Sept. 3, 2018.

Xi Jinping went personally to the countryside, to the villages, had people look at each individual, each family in poverty, to determine exactly what was needed to improve their condition. China is integrating the BRI with the African Union's Agenda 2063, a very, very beautiful and ambitious program which announced in 2013 that Africa will be fully modernized by 2063, a 50-year perspective to transform the African continent completely.

Xi Jinping said very clearly, the aim of all of this is to make the world more balanced and a better place for everyone to live in.

Let's listen to what the Africans themselves are saying. South Africa's President Cyril Ramaphosa said that China and Africa are entering a new golden age, a fantastic age of deep cooperation, based on equality, with deep respect for each other. He said the accusation of neocolonialism, which is being made against China, is propagated by people who envy us and who are jealous of our relationship. I think that that is absolutely true.

In his speech to the FOCAC summit in Beijing, Ramaphosa said: "Africa is independent now and is free to choose its partners. And China has been supportive and engaged in partnership where we are trying now to promote and assist each other."

So this is a historic break: 500 years of colonialism, 50, 70 years of IMF conditionalities suppressing Africa's development, is over, and the artificial keeping of Africa backward through the doctrines of physical economic stagnation, zero growth, and British-style free trade—which was imposed by the colonial powers on Africa—is over.

China is using today what President Franklin D. Roosevelt called, in his 1941 encounters with Britain's Prime Minister Churchill, "20th-century methods" meaning industrialization, increasing the productivity of labor power, increasing longevity, letting everyone in on the progress of science and technology, health,

ficial end of colonialism: It has given the African nations a great sense of empowerment, because China is offering them not only infrastructure investment, science and technological transfer, but also a strategy of leapfrogging, whereby African countries and other developing countries can have access to the most advanced science and technology, so as not to need to repeat all the levels of development of the West.

What Xi Jinping said at this conference is that China and Africa will "walk together towards prosperity. We will think with one mind, and work with one heart." China pledged $60 billion for projects in Africa over the next three years. And he also declared this is open to all nations—to the United States, to the Europeans, to Japan, to anybody who wants to participate.

China is synergizing the Belt and Road Initiative, already a global network of infrastructure, realizing what the Schiller Institute put out in its two reports, *The New Silk Road Becomes the World Land-Bridge*, volumes one and two, and the UN's Agenda 2030, which is the idea that poverty will be eradicated on the entire planet. China has taken a leading role in pushing that agenda forward, and China has the plan to eliminate poverty in China, altogether, by 2020. Now, that's less than two years from now, and they are on a very good track to accomplish exactly that.

Japanese Prime Minister Shinzo Abe (left), Chinese President Xi Jinping (center), and Russian President Vladimir Putin at the Eastern Economic Forum in Vladivostok, Russia, Sept. 12, 2018.

infrastructure and so forth; not "18th-century methods," meaning looting, exploitation, slave trade, exploiting raw materials. There is a new saying, that "Africa is becoming the new China, but the new China with African characteristics." China entered into a Memorandum of Understanding with 37 countries at this FOCAC meeting. This is a complete explosion of development.

One week later, the Eastern Economic Forum convened in Vladivostok, Russia, representing a similar gigantic, strategic realignment in the direction of development, with 6,000 participants from 60 nations: 3,000 Russians, 1,000 Chinese, many people from South Korea, North Korea, Japan. Participants discussed making Russia's Siberia and Far East the new frontier of the East. Remember that this is one of the largest regions of untapped resources of the world, because in the Far East of Russia, there are all the Elements of the Mendeleyev Table in large quantities. So, if you have joint investment from North and South Korea, from Japan, from Russia and from other nations to develop this region—in which the United States could easily participate via the Bering Strait, and connect to the trans-Eurasian network—it brings a lot of prosperity to many people on the planet for decades to come.

Very exciting at this summit, was the announcement by President Putin and Prime Minister Shinzo Abe of Japan that there will be a peace treaty between their two countries by the end of the year, finally ending the de facto state of not-war, but no peace treaty, between the two countries. I'm planning very much to pick up on that, demanding a peace treaty be concluded between the United States and Germany—which I think is also very, very urgent.

So what I want you to grasp,— that you not think that the reality is what you see here inside the United States. You are living in a fishbowl, a completely artificial environment, where you have no chance to know about the real issues going on in the world and determining the future of mankind, if you rely on the mass media. If you don't know what you're looking for, even the Internet doesn't help you, because the Internet floods you with "information," all these apps and messages and so forth, but you have to know what you are looking for. If you take my remarks here as a guideline, you will be able to find the proof.

There is a new system, a completely new paradigm of relations among nations developing, and as Prime Minister Abe at the Vladivostok meeting said, we have to get rid of everything of the postwar period, we need a completely new beginning.

Everything I am saying to you is contradicted by the mainstream media and the think tanks that for about four years have ignored all of these fantastic developments. And all of a sudden, however, they woke up and realized that this is all happening. So, they started an unprecedented slander campaign against the New Silk Road, saying this is luring the third world countries into a debt trap. Now, nothing could be less true: China is forgiving many of the loans it has made, while it is the Western countries that have caused a debt trap for many of the developing countries. Another of their arguments is, "China is proceeding with neocolonialism." Well, I'm sorry: If China is uplifting living standards, with giving fair conditions of equal treatment and win-win cooperation, this is the opposite of colonialism.

Another argument: "They're only deploying Chinese labor, there is no transparency. These projects are not profitable, they are creating dependency for the Third World." Well, I would advise people to read the June 2017 McKinsey report on Chinese economic engagement in Africa, which shows that Chinese investments in Africa are all to the benefit of the receiving countries: they are for the first time giving Africa a de-

Xinhua/Chen Cheng

Chinese-financed Mombasa-Nairobi Standard Gauge Railway (SGR) arrives at Nairobi Terminus.

velopment chance; they are deploying 90% African labor; only those positions which the Africans are not trained for are temporarily taken over by the Chinese. In Ethiopia, for example, China is now setting up an academy for people to learn how to run sophisticated, fast railways, giving their knowledge to many millions of other people.

The McKinsey report also states that these projects are not following a big master plan, where the Chinese Communist government controls every investment, but that all of these investments basically follow market rules—and McKinsey is not exactly your Communist propaganda outfit.

At stake here is the image of man. China says, Xi Jinping says, that the African continent has the biggest development potential in all the world, because they need the most development. By the year 2050, Africa will have 2.5 billion people. That means, you will have a lot of young people; Africa will be the youngest continent of all. If the young people of Africa are properly educated, they will be the most prosperous. This is in complete contrast to the image of man, for example, given by the author Stephen Smith, a lecturer at Duke University here in the United States, who wrote an absolutely horrific book which is being quoted everywhere right now in the Western media. The title of this book is *EurAfrica: Young Africa Comes to the Old Continent* [*La Ruée vers l'Europe: La Jeune Afrique en route vers le Vieux Continent*].

Referring to the migrant crisis in Europe, Smith writes that Chinese investments in Africa are terrible, and are the reason for the migrant crisis, because they allow Africans to have a certain living standard, so that then they have the means to come to the European continent or drown in the Mediterranean. It's completely crazy! But this nonsense is being quoted everywhere. And if you look at the language in this book, it is the old Rockefeller mantra: overpopulation, youth surplus, excess youth—all completely cynical and anti-human words! As if human beings were some kind of parasite of which there are too many. Quite incredible!

So on the other hand, China and Africans are emphasizing that what unites them is a deep friendship. Winston Churchill said that such relationships are completely impossible, because between countries, you can't have friendship, you only have "interests." With a neo-liberal, neo-con establishment, that is ob-

Xinhua/Michael Tewelde

Ethiopian and Djiboutian trainees attend a training session in Addis Abeba, capital of Ethiopia, July 9, 2018.

viously true. But if you reach out and have a people-to-people understanding, if you respect the beautiful culture of the other country, you can develop love! You can develop friendship, because you realize that God has made the world so multiply-beautiful that once you know all of these other cultures, you are enriched. Xi Jinping says the aim of all of this is happiness for all.

The geopolitical faction is used to thinking in terms of geopolitics. It's either the U.S. interests or the European Union interests against China, against Russia; in Europe, meanwhile, it's against the United States: They engage in these geopolitical spectacles, to induce you to think that these are the only actions to take, leaving it impossible, they hope, for you to imagine that mankind is capable of creating a completely different system of human relations.

One example of the difference in thinking—and I thought that this was one of the most beautiful occasions to see that difference—was the answer Xi Jinping gave recently in response to a letter from eight senior professors of the Central Academy of Fine Arts in Beijing, in which these professors asked him, "How much significance do you give to the question of the aesthetical education?" Xi Jinping said that aesthetical education in great Classical arts in the training of students has the highest importance, because the goal of this aesthetical education is to create beautiful minds.

In the tradition of Friedrich Schiller, that happens to be one of the absolute aims of the Schiller Institute. We want people to develop beautiful souls! For Schiller, beautiful soul and mind is very much the same.

Now, think about how the youth in American are being treated. The drug epidemic, the suicide rate, the despair, the non-idea of a future, and you could not see more clearly the problem. I think President Trump knows that; he has already said he wants to get rid of this drug epidemic, but the present battles he is involved in have made it very difficult for him to do that.

Look at the changes in the world: Russia and China are now in a strategic alliance. At the Vladivostok summit they are deepening their regional cooperation according to the Volga-Yangtze mechanism. At the same time, Russia, for the first time with China, has conducted very large joint military maneuvers in Russia's Far East. So, you see the two potentials: It's very clear Russia and China are building a new world, but they're also making very clear, they're not going to be pushed over. They're not going to start a war, but they also make very clear, they know how to defend themselves.

So, I think people in the West have to make up their minds: Either we in the West—the United States and Europe—join the new paradigm, or we go in the direction of confrontation, which, should it escalate into actual warfighting, in all likelihood would mean the annihilation of civilization. That is really *the* issue of the midterm elections. It's not what people think—this or that—it is *this*, and I fully agree with Willy Wimmer, that what stands between all of us and World War III, is Donald Trump. Should he be driven out of office, one way or another, I would not give two pennies for world peace.

Look at the hysteria being expressed by certain Democrats, who used to be reasonable in the past. They have gone completely mad! I mean, one example for me, is Robert Reich, who when he was Labor Secretary in the Clinton Administration used to say sometimes quite decent things on economics. But in a recent editorial, he wrote that we have to annihilate Trump! This Presidential election should be annihilated from the memory of history, it should never have happened! You don't talk like that, unless you are possessed and driven, and many of these people have said similar things.

Solution to Imminent World Financial Blowout

There is one other danger: And that is that ten years after the financial crash of 2008, we are again at a point of a potential explosion of the monetary system, but on a much larger scale. William White, the former chief economist of the Bank for International Settlements, who is a quite good economist—we have studied his works for quite some time—just came out saying that since none of the causes of the 2008 crash have been removed, the world could witness a financial blowout at any moment. Jean-Claude Trichet, former president of the European Central Bank (ECB) from 2003-2011, just said the same thing: the danger is of a blowout. Many others are warning that a financial blowout could occur way before the midterm elections in the United States.

Were a financial blowout to happen, the world could end up in chaos, and out of chaos would come war. As a remedy, Trichet is prescribing more of the poison he spread when he was at the ECB, namely, more "structural reforms," more austerity, more reduction of wages and similar things.

But there actually is a solution. We are now at the

William White, chief economist of the Bank for International Settlements, 1995-2008.

Jean-Claude Trichet, President of the European Central Bank, 2003-2011.

point warned about in a video by Mr. LaRouche on July 25, 2007, one week before the secondary mortgage crisis in the United States broke out, where he said the financial system is hopelessly bankrupt and nothing in the world can be done to undo that, unless you completely reform it and go for Glass-Steagall, go for a New Bretton Woods system. He said that everything we see now will be just the different aspects of this bankrupt system coming to the surface—which then happened in 2007 with the mortgage crisis and 2008 and the Lehman Brothers bankruptcy filing, the largest in U.S. history.

Since the central banks did absolutely nothing to remedy that, we have now a situation where corporate debt, indebtedness in general is at an all-time high. When the Federal Reserve tried to increase the interest rate just a little bit, the currencies of the "emerging market" countries started to go down, practically without a bottom; so, you have a minefield which could lead to a complete explosion in the next weeks.

China is well aware of all this. They have for some time demanded a new financial international governance; they have introduced a new law forbidding speculation and actually forbidding Chinese investors from involving their money in international speculative activity. This is one of the various things one has to consider in light of the U.S. trade war against China, the U.S. sanctions against Russia, the secondary sanctions against Europeans who are affected by these sanctions. In many parts of the world already there is talk about replacing the dollar as a world leading currency, and instead conducting trade with national currencies, for example the Turkish lira, the Russian ruble, the Chinese yuan/renminbi.

The problem is, such schemes won't work without the United States being included in a proposed solution, all these beautiful efforts by other countries to establish different relations may not work, because with chaos reigning in the trans-Atlantic financial system, I do not think the United States would agree to its own demise in the same peaceful way that the Soviet Union eventually did when it disintegrated in 1991. Given the dangers under conditions of a general breakdown chaos, I think the potential is great for the United States to go into a civil war. Many European analysts have warned about such a possibility recently, given the incredible degree of weaponry in the country, automatic rifles and so forth. But at the same time, the United States could very well engage in a large war on a global scale.

This is why the only way out—and this has been said by my husband many years ago—is to have a New Bretton Woods, to go back to where Nixon went in the wrong way on Aug. 15, 1971, when he decoupled the dollar from gold and dissolved the fixed exchange rate system, which was really the beginning of this absolutely excessive deregulation of the markets, leading to the present casino economy. We must go back to that point, go back to a fixed exchange rate system, but you have to improve it, which is why it has to be called a "New" Bretton Woods.

While Franklin D. Roosevelt had one intention, as I mentioned earlier, namely, to use "20th-century methods" to end colonialism in the developing countries, under Harry Truman, the Bretton Woods system became very much influenced by Churchill's views, and this is why, when you talk about New Bretton Woods, many people in Africa and other countries say, "Oh no! We don't want that, because it put us at so much of a disadvantage!" Which is why we are saying a *New* Bretton Woods: Because you need to have a kind of return to a system where it is not the maximum profit of the speculators, but the common good of the people which must be the purpose of economy.

My husband has said many times—and if you think about it, it makes absolute sense—that in order to get rid of the power which rules the West right now, that is, the City of London and its Wall Street satrapy, which are really also behind all the war provocations and behind many

Xinhua/Li He

A Fuxing bullet train leaves Beijing South Railway Station on the Beijing-Shanghai high-speed railway, with a maximum speed of 350 kph.

other evil things, the only way to overpower them is with a Four Power agreement. You need a combination of the United States, China, Russia and India, possibly with Japan, with an open invitation to all other nations. But you need that initiating core combination which is powerful enough to replace the system of the British Empire with an international credit system, based on the American system of economy of Alexander Hamilton.

This combination must start with a banking separation by implementing a global Glass-Steagall; then create a national bank in each country, thus returning to the sovereign states and governments the power of credit generation; have the newly established national banks issue massive amounts of credit for physical economic construction; and set up a global system of governance based on a commitment to cooperation among sovereign nations.

A New Bretton Woods system, as intended by FDR, would develop the developing countries, but not with "20th-century methods" but with 21st-century methods by allowing these countries to leapfrog to a level of complete development, by increasing their productivity, living standards, longevity and allow them to participate in the fruits of science and technology on the highest level.

U.S. Potholes and Tolls, China's High-Speed Rail

Some may say, "This is utopian, this cannot happen." But that's not true! The framework for this already exists, in the form of the Belt and Road Initiative becoming the World Land-Bridge. There already exists a global cooperation network connecting continents through corridors, tunnels, bridges, by air, by land, by sea. It all began when China embarked on building the infrastructure that the world suffers so much from a lack of. There is a tremendous lack of infrastructure, not only in the developing countries, but also in the West. Having come this morning from New Jersey to New York, I can emphatically say "especially in the United States!" I don't know, frankly, how you do this, you know. [laughter]

How can you travel on these roads, which have such potholes—you know, if you have a back problem, every two meters you experience a shock to your bones; but also, people are rageful, it's dangerous. Two hours in the morning, two hours in the evening, in some cases even more. It's irrational to the hilt! It's completely crazy! I don't understand why you don't make a riot about it, saying: "We don't want this! This is cheating us of our lives!"

Compare your highways and railways with the fast train system in China. If ever you have any tourist plans, go to China, travel on their fast train system. They go by now at 320-330 kph, about 200 mph. They're smooth, they fly through the landscape. They're quiet; they don't shake, because they're built very well. China's building a fast train between all major cities in China. The one from Shanghai to Beijing takes a little bit less than five hours. To Nanjing, four hours.

They're now taking an area the size of New York and New Jersey—namely the triangle between Beijing,

Tientsin, and Hebei province—and they're revamping the whole thing, putting in fast trains; for the inner-city transport, slow maglev trains which go only 150 kph (93 mph), which can stop very quickly. The beautiful thing about the maglev, is that they have an extremely fast acceleration, so it takes only 10 seconds to attain full speed, as you're pushed into your seatback. The technology is such that it takes off and you're right there, and you can stop again. So, for inner-city traffic this is absolutely perfect.

This is what you need in the United States, a transport system connecting Philadelphia, Boston, New York, Chicago, Detroit, the West Coast, Texas, through a network of fast train systems. Your road system is outmoded! America has 250 km of fast train rail! Somewhere between New York and Boston, there is, I think, a little strip of 200 km where you can go at 250 kph, but that's all. So, you have *none, nothing!* You should get some high-speed rail built! [applause]

Serious, large-scale infrastructure cannot be built by private interests. Private investors need relatively quick return on their money. They tend to go for tolls on highways. Toll booths—to get from New Jersey to Manhattan, by car via the Lincoln Tunnel. If you pay cash, its $15, and then you pay $8 for another stretch. There are now places on the Capital Beltway around Washington, where at certain hours of the day, you pay $40 for a few miles! This is insane! What this means is, obviously, not everybody can afford that, so then many cars go off the highway, take side roads, which become congested, and it's completely suffocating the real economy. So the toll system is another one of these insane things, because infrastructure as such is not supposed to bring profit, but it's supposed to be the framework and environment for industry to blossom.

Ditch Trade War for Four Power Agreement

This is where we have to really get a mobilization going, because I think President Trump probably intends the right thing by imposing tariffs on certain categories of industry, like steel, aluminum, and other things. And I think he has a right impulse to undo the mistakes of previous administrations which have outsourced production to cheap labor markets. But the tariffs are not the right thing to do. I try to defend Trump, and I'm probably one of only two people in Germany who even dares to talk about the importance of Trump not losing the election—but I think here, he's really wrong. Because, if you want to have a Four Power

agreement, if you want to have friendship among the United States, Russia, China, India, and other countries, you cannot start a trade war.

Many Chinese I have recently spoken with are extremely upset, saying this is hurting everybody: It's hurting the U.S. consumers, who have to pay increased prices; it is not leading to the kind of technological innovation in new industries in the United States; and it is just plain punitive—the tariffs are being perceived as punitive against especially high-technology areas, as a means to stop China from reaching its China 2021 goals. This is causing bad blood, and it brings to mind the "Thucydides trap." Will the United States allow the rise of China, or will a new world war come out of it? And that's how many people in China look at it.

There is, in my view, a much better way, namely, with the Four Power agreement to set up a New Bretton Woods system, to create a new credit mechanism, and then have Chinese invest in the infrastructure in the United States. China holds about $1 trillion in U.S. Treasury bonds. China's offer, made by Prime Minister Li Keqiang, has been that China could use these Treasuries to invest in infrastructure in the United States and offer joint ventures in other countries, i.e., increase the size of the cake: And by increasing trade, get rid of the balance that way. Obviously, this is not liked by some people, but it is the rational solution.

Is it possible to get such an agreement? What people also don't consider, is that the Chinese economic model is very close to the American System of economy. Friedrich List, a collaborator of Mathew and Henry Carey, spent several years in the United States, and he wrote many works about the difference between the American and the British systems of economy. It happens to be that he is, right now, according to a 2011 article in the *Frankfurter Allgemeine Zeitung*, and many other reports, the most popular economist theoretician in China. The American journalist and author Chalmers Johnson noted the fact that List has much more influence in Asia, than *either* Adam Smith or Karl Marx. And the China model can actually be called a "neo-Hamiltonian" or "neo-Listian model with Chinese characteristics."

Were the President of the United States—who said he likes the American System of economy, and plans to implement Glass-Steagall—to agree to participate, the United States could engage in investment in high-tech exports to the countries of the Belt and Road Initiative. And even if these exports would not always bring the biggest profit, such activity would foster increased rates of technological turnover in the most advanced capital goods sector of production inside the United States, causing a continuous wave of innovation, and that way, increase the overall productivity of the U.S. economy.

As a byproduct of such exports, the U.S. would rapidly reverse the ill effects of outsourcing of production and deindustrialization. And, since the fastest rates of growth are found in space research and exploration, and joint space travel is the joint future mission of humanity, we should concentrate on development of the Moon and Mars, and unite us as humanity in this way.

Look Back From the Future

So, we have to change the way we think. Don't think from inside the box. If you look at German politics from inside Germany, you'd think you were in an insane asylum. Far too many people will tell you, "This is my position against your position," and they'll debate totally meaningless issues. I hate to tell you, but in the United States it looks pretty much the same way.

Think how humanity should look in 100 years from now. Today's vision of sending astronauts to the Moon and Mars will soon be realized. It's not a question of "if" but "when." So, let's concentrate on questions like, how can we create conditions to live on the ISS, to live in villages on the Moon, and then, eventually, on Mars.

We should think of today as us in the present, from the standpoint of Schiller's universal history: How would we like to be looked at from the standpoint of our grandchildren and great-grandchildren? Are we that force, that generation which initiated and contributed to the transformation of the world into a new paradigm, which ended colonialism, and which got mankind's history into the idea of the one humanity?

Coming back to the idea of the *punctum saliens* in history, that jumping point, that point of decision where all the moral potential is called forth, to not end up in a tragedy, but to create a new, more beautiful period of human civilization, this is presently our situation. So, with this purpose in our hearts and minds, let us work from the standpoint of a New Silk Road Spirit, to become truly human, and let that, in the sense of Percy Shelley, become the true spirit of the age.

Thank you.

Italy and China Cooperate To Develop Africa

From Liliana Gorini, Chairwoman of MoviSol, LaRouche Movement in Italy

Sept. 12—In the last weeks, thanks in part to the campaign of the Schiller Institute on the Belt and Road Initiative and the Transaqua plan for Lake Chad—which saw the first direct cooperation between Italy and China in the development of Africa—we have been in the middle of many initiatives of the Italian government and others in favor of closer cooperation between Italy and China to develop Africa. In this way we also contribute to the solution of the refugee problem, in which Italy has been left alone by the European Union.

Italian Finance and Economics Minister Giovanni Tria was in China for an important mission, and gave an interview to CGTN, in which he explained that Italy and China have many complementarities and can develop synergies in infrastructure investments, technologies, food, and aerospace. Italy is the second largest manufacturer in Europe and the seventh in the world. China is quickly developing high-quality industry and technology. We can put those technologies together and operate together in China, Italy and also third countries.

African countries should be a prime target of such cooperation, as was underscored by Undersecretary of State for Economic Development Michele Geraci, who created a Task Force China in the Ministry in Rome. In an interview with formiche.net, Geraci explained that Chinese investments in Africa have a return for us Italians because it helps to stabilize countries where our companies are active. Furthermore, I believe, it is a duty for an advanced country such as ours, not so much to host those who flee from the African continent, but to help Africans to not be compelled to leave their own lands. It is the only win-win solution for everybody.

In an article for *Global Times* two days ago Fabio Massimo Parenti, Associate Professor of International Studies at the International Institute Lorenzo de' Medici, in Florence, wrote that "Europe and China must come together for Africa." Cooperating with China on the Maritime Silk Road—which involves the Italian ports of Genoa, Trieste and Venice—will also be the key to relaunching commercial activities in Genoa, which has been hit badly by the collapse of the Morandi Bridge, which killed 43 people, the result of budget cuts and lack of maintenance.

I therefore wish full success to your important conference in New York, which is key not only for the United States, but also for Europe and Italy.

The United States Must Help Save Africa

From Ramasimong Phillip Tsokolibane, leader of LaRouche South Africa

Sept. 11—Dear Ladies and Gentlemen, gathered in New York City to discuss the way forward, that we might emerge from these turbulent and crisis-wracked times, into the bright light of a new and better future for all mankind,— I send you greetings and best wishes for the success of your efforts from South Africa, a proud member of the BRICS alliance for peace through development.

I want to convey to you this afternoon two important, inter-related points.

First, it should clear, that with the developments of the last several weeks, the world no longer needs to exist under the foot of the bitch Queen and her globally extended British Empire. There is a pathway towards a new paradigm that rejects the basic assumption of imperialism—that there are two castes of people, the first consisting of those pre-ordained to be masters, and a lower caste—of those considered by the first caste as less than human, enslaved by birth and circumstance to service the masters. This pathway to a new world has been laid out in discussions and plans by our BRICS partners, China, Russia and India, with the extensive assistance of my country's former president, Jacob Zuma, who was a committed, outspoken advocate of not only South Africa's development, but the development of the continent as a whole, and who led South Africa to play an important role in the BRICS.

The focus of the BRICS on Africa is not from the standpoint of looting and exploiting its people and resources for some "master race," but from the standpoint of development in the self-interest of Africans. Africans will no longer tolerate being treated as useless eaters, whose existence is permitted only so long as we can be exploited, and once that is finished, we should be eliminated by a combination of grinding poverty, wars, famine and disease. That is the way of all imperialisms; that it is the way of the British Empire. That way is now past.

Not so long ago in this world there were only two real "blocs," if you want to call them that, for want of a better term. The first bloc consisted of the imperialists and those who promoted their inhuman system of exploitation, playing nations and peoples against each other, whose ultimate aim was to reduce the population of this world to a billion people or less, as this was once expressed by his Royal Virus, Prince Phillip. The second bloc was made up of the nations and peoples being exploited.

My second point is that under the leadership of especially China's President Xi Jinping, author of the Belt and Road Initiative, with support and additional efforts of Russia's President Vladimir Putin, there is now a new way to look at the world. There is now a growing number of nations and national leaderships that reject the zero-sum games of imperialism's geopolitics and believe there is no reason we cannot have a global grand design, in which all nations and peoples are dedicated to the improvement of the general welfare and well-being of all peoples—where there are no losers, only winners on the road to progress.

This revolutionary thinking now stands opposed to the British Empire and its system of exploitation. At this moment, when the Empire's financial system is so fragile—when its system of profit-taking at the expense of human flesh is in an existential crisis—it is possible to throw off that system of oppression, and relegate it to the dustbin of history. Such a moment as this, in which fundamental change is possible, when the crumbling of the old social order encourages enough people to summon forth a new-found courage within themselves to challenge that order and seek something better, does not often occur. We are, right now, living in such an exciting moment, a moment of the kind the Polish revolutionary and economist Rosa Luxemburg called a "conjunctural crisis." And in the manner of the great Russian strategist Vladimir Lenin, we must "seize the moment."

Here's how I look at this. The British and their accomplices globally are embarked on a dread policy that pushes towards global war, in order to save their power.

Should they get their way—should they not be resisted, should nations and their peoples succumb to the British lies and behave as brainwashed zombies—then the lords will indeed "succeed" in reducing Earth's population, in short order, to around a billion people—a genocide that would have made the British golem, Adolf Hitler, blush with envy. This insane plan presumably spares the so-called 1%, or around 75 million masters, plus all those whom they might need to service their interests. Around a billion people or less—that is, if they don't miscalculate and kill *everyone* in a general thermonuclear war. As an African, I know, either way, I am toast.

China, and Russia, along with India—our BRICS partners—have done some heavy lifting to create the possibility of a new paradigm, extending credit directly and through such institutions as the BRICS New Development Bank, aimed at the building up the economy, both social and physical, that improves the creative productive powers of labour. This extension of credit is not intended to make monetary profit for the issuers. The Brits cannot comprehend this. Credit extended with the intent of productive development, builds a future, and is thus self-liquidating. Monetarist debt, as issued in the British system, is usury, plain and simple, whose intention is to loot and enslave, and ultimately cannibalize the debtor.

For more than a half century, Lyndon LaRouche, the leader of the global movement that I represent in South Africa, and his wife Helga, have fought tirelessly against the British Empire and its monetarist system of imperial looting. They have led us to a policy of peace through improvement of the creative powers of all people alive, and for those untold generations yet unborn—a globally extended, expanded reproduction of our species, with greater numbers at ever higher levels of creative and productive potential. That work has placed the nations of the BRICS alliance, most prominently China, Russia, and India, behind the idea of a new era for mankind, without geopolitical imperial wars and conflict.

Meanwhile, Africa has worked diligently, and with great effort, to put itself in a position to benefit from the course taken by the BRICS and its allies. That is shown, for example, by the dramatic concord at the just-concluded summit of the Forum on China-Africa Cooperation in Beijing, where the African nations collectively committed themselves to China's Belt and Road Initiative. Africa's leadership recognizes that such development programmes represent the only hope to raise its people from the murderously enforced underdevelopment of the British imperial system.

I conclude, with a final point. This new paradigm

cannot be realized without the active support and full collaboration of the United States.

I am speaking now directly to the Americans in your audience: Your nation was founded on the two inter-related self-evident principles. First, that all men are created fundamentally equal by our Creator; and second, that governments are instituted among men to serve the best interests of all people, offering opportunities to realize their full creative potential, not by serving the interests of an imperial or any elite, but by providing conditions to promote their general welfare. Your great American President Franklin Roosevelt believed that, to secure the blessings of peace and prosperity of the American people, this principle of the General Welfare must be extended to all nations and all people.

Your President, Donald Trump, is being savaged, in an ongoing attack by the British Empire, which seeks a coup and regime change in your own country, such as it has accomplished elsewhere, with the help of its assets such as the Queen's own lawn jockey, Barack Obama. I have invited Mr. Trump to visit my country and Africa generally, so that he may see for himself the damage, destruction and death wrought by British imperial policy, but also the great possibilities for change for the better. Africa needs Donald Trump to move America to stand with our friends the Chinese, Russians, and Indians, and thus create the Four-Power combination that Mr. LaRouche has said must be created, and thereby assert America's desire and power to create a new and just global economic system to replace the decadent and dying British-dominated world order—joining with other nations to usher in a new era of peace through development. In that lies Africa's salvation, as it does for the rest of the world.

So, I urge all of you who are Americans: To save Africa, you must defeat the British Empire and its plans to save the 1%, and to do that you must defeat the efforts to destroy Donald Trump and his Presidency! The Presidency of the United States is the most powerful institution on our planet. It was created by America's founding fathers for just such a moment as this.

And to your President, Donald Trump, I say: Do not fail us! Make America great by finally defeating its historic enemy, the enemy of all mankind—the British Empire! Purge yourself of its vile agents and assets, join ranks with us now, and we will walk, together, into a bold, new future.

Thank you!

Every Step of Syrian Reconstruction Is a Celebration of the New Silk Road

From Ulf Sandmark, Leader of the LaRouche movement in Sweden

A full report on the Schiller Institute delegation of Odile Mojon and Ulf Sandmark to Syria is included elsewhere in this issue. Sandmark's greetings here are correspondingly abbreviated.

We are happy to report to you that we toured a major part of Syria, including the cities of Homs, Aleppo and Palmyra. We saw the shocking devastation brought upon huge areas of these cities by madmen sent by our own nations into homes, schools, hospitals, industry, and precious ancient sites that are part of the universal heritage of mankind.

Every child in Syria knows about the ugly staging of chemical attacks as a way to bring even more aggression. Indian journalists we met told us that the western nations supporting terrorists in Syria have broken with every principle of Human Rights in their wars against West Asia. It has gone so far that films with white people as the crooks are now popular there.

The Schiller Institute is opposing this geopolitical war and is fighting for reconstruction and development. We were very well received in two live interviews on national Syrian TV, as we spoke about our worldwide mobilization to spread the statements of Helga Zepp-LaRouche, encourage the phone calls to the White House, and support the actions of Virginia State Senator Richard Black, the Veteran Intelligence Professionals for Sanity (VIPS) and other allies in this cause.

Every step of Syrian reconstruction is a celebration of the New Silk Road. Especially the impressive 60th Damascus International Trade Fair, which we visited and where we saw the reunion of the old Silk Road nations.

Syrian reconstruction is everywhere to be seen, and we met great operational interest in our proposals as published in our two World Land-Bridge reports, volume 1 and volume 2.

Only a Four Power Agreement Can Prevent War, Assure Development

The Belt and Road: World Cooperation for the Benefit of All

by Dr. Xu Wenhong

Dr. Xu Wenhong is Senior Research Fellow, Center for One Belt One Road, Chinese Academy of Social Sciences, in Beijing, China. This is an edited transcript of his remarks to the New York Schiller Institute Conference, September 13, 2018. EIR has provided the title. Dr. Xu spoke via pre-recorded video.

Schiller Institute

Dr. Xu Wenhong

Dear Mme. Helga LaRouche, dear participants of this forum, Ladies and Gentlemen, good afternoon!

I am very honored to speak to you today about China's One Belt, One Road Initiative. Many thanks to the organizers for this kind invitation.

As we all know, for the past four decades, the world has been watching China's unprecedented economic growth. Now, we know that the secret of China's rapid rise: The panacea consists of a peaceful and stable environment, investment in infrastructure construction, close regional and global cooperation, integration of worldwide resources, creating collaboration, better access to education and closer people-to-people exchanges. That's why the rest of the world was counting on China during the international financial crisis starting from 2008. China has become the second largest economy on the planet since 2010. Expectations for its performance on the world stage have been ever increasing.

China boasts a different philosophy and cultural tradition from most other countries and regions in the world. The Chinese people believe that when you are impoverished, you should first discipline yourself; and when you get wealthy, you should bring benefits to others.

For the past four decades, China has lifted millions of its people out of poverty, which is indeed a marvelous success. Now, the world is seeing how the Belt and Road Initiative is helping millions in other countries shake off poverty.

Five years ago, the grand conception was first envisioned by Chinese President Xi Jinping, in an aim to revive the ancient Silk Road trading route, by inviting developing countries to share social-economic progress. Now, five years later, the majority of the countries involved in the Belt and Road Initiative have scored major progress through closer cooperation with China.

Cambodian women have found jobs in newly founded factories in Sihanoukville. An increasing number of entrepreneurs have moved into Great Stone [Industrial Park], the biggest joint project of Belarus and China, in Minsk. In Kenya, passengers can go from Mombasa to Nairobi in only 4.5 hours on Express Rail. More Greeks, struggling to make a living after the European debt crisis, have found new jobs in Piraeus Port.

Over the past five years, China has been upholding a fundamental belief that all cooperation projects should be built on the principles of transparency, inclusiveness, and sustainability. In the implementation of the Belt and Road Initiative, China has no intention to change the existing international system. Instead, it aims to cooperate with more nations within this framework to contribute to regional and global development. In this process, China has become a staunch supporter of globalization. China is playing an increasingly important role in anti-protectionism, especially against the backdrop of U.S. President Donald Trump's frenzy for trade skepticism. Now that unilateralism and populism are gaining traction, the Belt and Road Initiative inevitably has become a target of criticism from those with evil intentions and vested interests.

However, they should better see the fact that globalization is becoming irreversible and China is just one of many countries fighting to defend it. That's why we need more and more people to truly understand the significance of the Belt and Road Initiative, and to embrace the Belt and Road Initiative.

Through close cooperation along the Belt and Road, developing countries in Africa, Central Asia, and Southeast Asia have embraced more convenient transportation, better health care, and more access to education. For all the people who have a deep belief that all men are created equal, they have a chance of development along the modern Silk Road.

I sincerely wish you a successful forum. Thank you.

RICHARD BLACK

Reconciliation and Rebuilding in Syria, as a Great Battle Looms in Idlib

This is an edited extract of remarks by Virginia State Senator Richard Black to the Sept. 13, 2018 Schiller Institute Conference in New York. For a fuller report on his latest trip to Syria, see the interview conducted by William Wertz, elsewhere in this issue.

It's very good to be with you. I am just back from Syria; I was there from September 1 to 9. It was a tremendous trip. I covered a great deal of the country. I went all the way from Damascus to Aleppo and to other places in between.

This is the second trip that I have taken. I was over there two years ago, and at the time I went to the city of Palmyra. Palmyra had just been liberated from ISIS, so I paid the visit, and shortly afterwards ISIS counterattacked and seized Palmyra once again.

Things have changed enormously. I met for three hours with President Bashar al-Assad, who, contrary to mainstream media, is an extremely rational, highly intelligent, and I think a very decent individual. He was really almost joyous. He felt that peace was at hand, a

Schiller Institute

Virginia State Senator Richard Black.

feeling that was shared by people just across the country. Talking with shepherds out in the desert, they were all so delighted that the terrorists have been driven from Syria in almost every area, and were looking at returning to peace, having the refugees, having their relatives return, and then rebuilding the country.

**Syria Rebuilds,
Even as Idlib Battle Looms**

This was the spirit. You can see the country being rebuilt all over. And I'll tell you, the security—I had very, very light security—even though I travelled for five miles through open areas. Previously, when I travelled, I had to have a 12-vehicle convoy, with three automatic cannons, and air support, attack helicopters and a jet. This time, I had one carload of troops, and I don't think they were Syria's elite secret service.

This was a tremendous, positive change. Everything was going well while I was over there. Subsequently, what has happened is that the remaining terrorists, the worst of the worst, have been trapped in Idlib province. They are under the general command of a fellow named

Clearing out the rubble, preparing to rebuild. Aleppo, Syria, Sept. 9, 2018.

now fighting shoulder-to-shoulder with ISIS and with al-Qaeda, and we are putting out these wild claims that there's going to be a Syrian gas attack, another one of these false-flag gas attacks.

I think it's a tragedy. I wish that the people in New York City whose families died on 9/11 understood that we are now *fighting*, struggling—John Bolton is going around the world enlisting the support of the world to attack Syria and to defend al-Qaeda and ISIS in Syria! This is the situation that we face today. It is a bizarre situation, something that no American would ever expect after the trauma of 9/11. And so I'm hoping that as we get the word out, we make it more difficult for the deep state to engage us in an escalation of this seven-year, painful, brutal war in Syria.

Abu Mohammed al-Julani, the top commander of Al-Nusra, which is al-Qaeda in Syria.

Let me remind you: Al-Qaeda was the group that flew the planes into the Twin Towers and the Pentagon on 9/11, killing 3,000 Americans. The commander of this force is al-Julani; he also is a major commander for ISIS in Nineveh province. He has taken command of Idlib province where a great battle is looming. The Syrian army has surrounded it and is set to move in and crush the greatest terror army on Earth.

The civilians within Idlib are desperate to be liberated. Many of them have escaped and gotten out. The Christians there are being ferreted out and beheaded whenever they can be detected. Some people talk about the "families" of the terrorists, saying "Well, we have to show great sympathy toward the terrorists' families." What we need to recognize is that typically, the "wife" of a terrorist is a slave. She has been captured in battle, and the rule that the terrorists follow is that a woman who is captured—she, her daughters, her children—are sex slaves, and they are traded back and forth among the terrorists.

Here we are. I think I and the rest of the world—the rest of the informed world—are shocked that here we are right around the time of the anniversary of 9/11, and we have thrown our full diplomatic and military weight in support of al-Qaeda. We are

A Policy of Reconciliation

One of the policies that has been followed by President Assad has been reconciliation. There's a bureau of reconciliation and they talk with rebels in various towns, and they get them to surrender their weapons, and in exchange they're given amnesty. Those who have not fought on behalf of the Syrian army, actually join and fight on the front lines.

I was extremely skeptical. When I first heard of this, I thought, all they're going to do is, they're going to act as though they're going along with it, and as soon as the opportunity arises, they'll stab the Syrian

Sen. Black being shown captured rebel barrel bomb munitions, Lieramon Factory, Syria, September 2018.

army in the back. In fact, the people of Syria have so turned against the war, now that they've had experience with these foreign jihadists that we have recruited from all around the world. (The United States recruits them, arms them, trains them, sends them off, and they man al-Qaeda, they man ISIS.) Many of these towns that joined the early revolution have said this stinks; this is not what we want. We want the old Syria that we had before.

From all reports that I can obtain, reconciliation has been a resounding success, and it has pacified the country. And for this reason, I was able to stop at obscure places. We'd be out in the desert and need to make a rest stop, and there'd be some little shanty, some fellow who would be growing a few olive trees, eking out a living, and we'd stop there. We weren't there to question them, we were there to use the restroom—and they would volunteer, and they would say: We are so delighted that the terrorists have been driven out and we want to express our gratitude to President Bashar al Assad. I have heard this from peasants, from people who sweep streets, who clean toilets for a living, all the way up to members of Parliament.

The Status of Women and Religion

I met with the head of Parliament and with a good portion of the Parliament of Syria, and I will tell you something that the mainstream media won't tell you: The Parliament has a substantial number of women who are the top legislators. We're always told that the Sunnis don't have any authority in Syria: The fact of the matter is that the President's wife is a Sunni, and she is very powerful, not only nationally but within her own family. The President's principal media and political advisor is Sunni. The Grand Mufti, who is the top Sunni authority in Syria and surrounding locations, is an ardent supporter of the President. Most of the Syrian generals are Sunni; most of the top officials in government are Sunni.

This whole myth [of religious conflict] was created as part of the justification for going to war against Syria—that somehow, we needed to figure out which religious group would control the country.

Reconciliation has been a very surprising success, and the country has clearly come together. There is enormous unity, and I think there's probably not a politician in the United States that would not die to have the popularity ratings of the President of Syria.

JAMES GEORGE JATRAS

It's Time for Us All To Escape from the 'Trans-Atlanticism' Straitjacket

This is an edited transcript of remarks by James George Jatras, former U.S. diplomat and former advisor to the Republican Senate leadership. He spoke to the Sept. 13, 2018 Schiller Institute Conference in New York via pre-recorded video.

Ladies and Gentlemen, this is Jim Jatras. I'm a former U.S. diplomat and longtime foreign policy advisor to the Senate Republican leadership. I'm honored to be invited to address this distinguished conference today. I thank Helga Zepp-

James George Jatras

LaRouche and the Schiller Institute, and all of the people who've made this event possible. I apologize, I'm not able to be there with you today in person, but I'm pleased to be able to talk to you remotely from this recorded statement.

I think it's fair to say, we live in one of those terrible historical junctures, where there really are two paths set out in front of us. One is the path of peace, prosperity, development, construction, the release of human potential; and the other one, is something comparable, I would say, not even to 1939, but rather comparable to 1914, with the world standing on the edge of an abyss, of a great global conflict with potential consequences that are unforeseen and foreseeable, but would be of a nature so destructive that we can't even imagine, as indeed, people in 1914 could not have imagined what was facing them.

Why Isn't U.S. Foreign Policy Based on Development?

As I understand, the main focus of this conference today is not the bad side, the bad things that could happen, but rather the constructive side of things, a New Bretton Woods, but one that is not based on a kind of an exploitive capital model, but rather, one that provides the kind of credit, the kind of development that we see, for example, in the Chinese involvement in Africa, and the One Belt, One Road Initiative of China.

It raises the question: Why has this not been the model going forward for the United States? I hope, with the recent announcement that the United States and Mexico are embarking on a new trade deal to replace the failed NAFTA agreement, that we will begin to see this kind of positive development here in the Western Hemisphere. One wonders why, instead of inveighing against the Russians and the Chinese or whoever it is, we're not thinking about here—we are here in the United States, in a wonderful position, in a wonderful hemisphere, which is brimming with possibilities for development. Our neighbors to the south—as well as Canada—but primarily our neighbors to the south could benefit from the same kind of initiative that we see the Chinese and the Russians and the Indians taking in Eurasia.

I do hope that this is at the core of President Donald Trump's vision for moving forward, that we can find some way to reach an accommodation with Moscow and China—and I would say, with India as well—on a stable, global order.

I am hoping for a global order that is not based on the vain and futile and destructive pursuit of a continued hegemony over the globe, that has been exercised in concert—and let's be honest about this—in concert with not only elements of the U.S. deep state, that have been trying for well over a year now to remove Donald Trump from office, but with their British counterparts, who I would say are at the very root of what is not merely foreign meddling—not Russian—British foreign meddling in our domestic affairs, in an attempt to corrupt our politics and to overthrow our constitutionally elected President. Instead of that, we can embark on more cooperative endeavors.

The Dangers of a Trump Impeachment

I think we need to be very realistic about the danger that confronts us, of the other path, the path to destruction. As I mentioned in regard to the British, ever since that Steele dossier, which has nothing to do with Russia as far as anybody can tell, you hear people on the American media, both pro- and anti-Trump, talking about Russian dirt, Russian lies in that dossier. As far as I know, there's nothing Russian about it: It's purely a part of the efforts by Christopher Steele, MI6 and British intelligence to try to queer the American election; to put GCHQ surveillance over the Trump campaign, and then to keep the pot boiling in some way that will result in Trump's impeachment.

And by the way, I don't take that as an idle possibility. I think there's a real danger that if the House goes Democrat in this election, Mr. Trump will be impeached. And if he is, despite the likelihood that Republicans will retain control of the Senate, I think there's a very good chance that he will be removed. There's a difference in mentality. Look, I worked in the Senate for over 17 years, I know how these people think. Unlike the Democrats who rallied around their President, Bill Clinton, and made sure that he was not removed, let's remember how Republican Senators were the ones that gave Nixon the heave-ho, and told him, if he did not resign, they would vote to have him removed.

I'm pretty sure, in my own mind, that if Trump were impeached by the House, on whatever the flimsy grounds might be, that a significant number of Republican Senators would jump at the chance to put Vice President Mike Pence in the Oval Office and Nikki Haley in as Vice President. And they would vote to remove Trump, although, unlike Nixon, I don't think he would resign.

I think we are really balancing on a knife's edge here, with regard to the political future of our country, and whether a positive vision of development, peace, and prosperity can be put in place, in lieu of what we've been dealing with for the last half-century or so, of trying to maintain this hegemonic global order.

War with Russia over Fake Chemical Attack?

The immediate danger I see, however, that faces us now, is in Syria. I was one of those who signed a recent statement that's found on *Consortium News* that's been distributed through other outlets, and I want to, again, thank the LaRouche organizations for helping get this statement of the Veteran Intelligence Professionals for Sanity (VIPS) around. This was a statement of a number of people who have an intelligence background primarily, or others like myself, with a military or diplomatic background, to warn against what we see being prepared, in broad daylight, now, of this provocation of a false chemical attack in Syria by the jihadists—by the terrorists, by the al-Qaeda groups that control Idlib province—to create a pretext for the United States and Britain and France to attack Syria.

And again, not to harp on this theme, but I think there's some real British fingerprints here. Karen Pierce, the British Representative to the United Nations, drew a connection the other day in her comments, between the Skripal poisonings—falsely blamed on Russia—in the United Kingdom, and also, the use of chemical weapons in Syria: It's the Russians using chemical weapons everywhere! Well, that's one way to look at it.

The other way to look at it, is we have a staged British provocation with the Skripals inside the United Kingdom, and we also have the British secret services supporting the so-called White Helmets, who are simply the PR arm of al-Qaeda inside Syria, and they're taking a leading role in this provocation—while the Russians have exposed what the leading role of Britain will be in this provocation. Everybody hears it, everybody sees it coming, and you can bet your bottom dollar that when it is unleashed—and unfortunately, I expect it to be unleashed—that the American, and British, and other world media will pick it up, without any examination, without any question, to say, "The Syrians have used chemical weapons in Syria again!"

What Does Trump Know?

The question is, what does Donald Trump know about this? On the two previous occasions when he's struck Syria with cruise missiles, many people took some comfort in the fact that he deliberately inflicted what were pinprick strikes, that essentially struck empty buildings, nothing of significance, as though he knew that these were fake chemical attacks, or were done as a provocation by the terrorists themselves, but felt somehow so pressured, so constrained, so besieged by this deep state network that, as I say, is at least binational—between Britain and the United States—that he felt he had no other choice but to launch these strikes.

That worries me, now, when we hear people around him—Secretary of State Mike Pompeo, National Security Advisor John Bolton, and others including Nikki Haley, of course—saying that if there is "another" use of chemical weapons, which, of course will also be false, that the response from the United States, Britain and France will be more "robust." There's even talk about striking Damascus, government targets, Russian and Iranian targets, even talk of a "decapitation strike" to kill Assad personally!

There seems to be a kind of, almost a giddy, recklessness among American policymakers with regard to the Russians. Let's remember when a number of Russian contractors—excuse me, "mercenaries"—contractors were killed near Deir ez-Zor several months ago, that you heard people on the news talking about, with a kind of a sanguinary glee, "Oh, we killed 200 Russians; that'll teach them!" All we have to do, is roll up that newspaper and hit that Russian dog on the snout, and he'll learn his lesson.

The Russians have massed their forces in the Eastern Mediterranean, too, and there's reason to suppose that having informed us, in good faith, that this was being planned, that if their forces are targetted, if Russians are killed, they will not take this lying down. One has to wonder, how many times are we going to come back to the verge of World War III, because we have this deep state, this—in my mind, unconstitutional, criminal conspiracy—surrounding the President, that is bound and determined, one way or the other, by hook or by crook, to maintain this aggressive global posture, to push on the Russians, push in the Black Sea, push in the Baltic, push in Syria, push in Ukraine, that can only lead to one outcome?

What Do You Know and What Will You Do?

I have to ask myself sometimes, in the years immediately leading up to 1914, those last peacetime years, say, from 1910 to 1913, how many people had any inkling that their lives were about to be forever changed, and for many of them, prematurely ended? I don't think they could have had that sense. There's a former German official, Willy Wimmer, who recently said that 2018 may go down in history as the last peacetime year—if there's anyone around to remember that. And I think the stakes are really that high.

I commend those gathered here today. I'm sorry I can't be with you in person. I think it is absolutely imperative to come to some agreement, some partnership, of the United States, Russia, China, India, and other countries, especially those involved in the Shanghai Cooperation Organization (SCO).

There's a real opportunity here, for people in Europe to escape from this so-called "trans-Atlanticism" straitjacket—which really just means a satellite status, from Washington—to recognize that their own national interests are all bound up in Eurasian integration, and the path of peace and prosperity that is being offered from the other side of the world. It is the one that I think our President really would like to follow, if he is able. But to what extent he is constrained, to what extent he is surrounded by people who only tell him things that are not true, I really don't know. And this is what worries me.

I thank all of you for listening to my brief remarks today. I hope all of us will raise our voices in any way we can, in support of a policy of peace, progress, development, and the release of human potential; and against the forces of destruction. Let's keep in mind the ever-increasing muzzling of independent voices online, which are the real alternative to the government-controlled, corporate media.

So again, thank you so much, and best wishes to all.

DMITRY POLYANSKIY

We Are Keen for Friendship and Economic Partnership, No Matter How Difficult It May Seem

This is an edited transcript of remarks by Dmitry Polyanskiy, First Deputy Permanent Representative of the Russian Federation's Permanent Mission to the United Nations.

Thank you so much! I'm really very honored to be here with all of you, discussing such important topics. Actually, we are discussing many of them in the Security Council. When you see very heated discussions, sometimes bordering on some insults, please don't believe that anything is so bad, because in the corridors, we have normal human relationships. I think that we are committed, all of us, including our American colleagues on the Security Council, to do everything to avoid the consequences of some political moves that can be unpredictable, and to avoid confrontation and military confrontation among superpowers.

Schiller Institute

Dmitry Polyanskiy

Things Aren't Always What They Seem

You know, we're living in a post-truth world, and a lot of things that are being said or done, or presented on TV or in the mass media, seem unrealistic, absurd, and they do not have very much in common with reality. It's very much like our work in the Security Council: So, you see something on the surface, and you say, "Oh, come on, Russia is struggling with the United States, they're not speaking with each other, they're sort of trading insults." But some things that are happening behind closed doors are more reassuring.

That's why I think we need to wait a little bit and to make this period of our relations pass away, because we know that there are a lot of clever people in America. We don't have problems with common Americans, they are very friendly, they are very intelligent, their attitude towards my country is very open, and we appreciate it very much. We have problems with some representatives of the political establishment—actually, almost all of them, [laughter] but that's how it happens. There are a lot of things being said that are not linked to the things on the ground; so, the on-the-ground situation is better. Yes, we have very difficult, harsh times in Syria, but we're still speaking with each other, and our military people are interacting. It's about our relations with the United States.

There is another track which is very assuring: I think we have very much advanced in building our partnership with China. The Eastern Economic Forum in Vladivostok is ongoing right now, and there were very important meetings between our leaders; a lot of contracts are being signed. Some commentators and analysts are saying that this is really a genuine start of Russian-Chinese economic partnership, first of all because there are so many threats coming from this part of the world, vis-à-vis my country and vis-à-vis China, that inevitably, we have to adjust our policies, we have to close ranks. This is not a friendship *against* somebody, it's sort of a win-win situation, as we see it.

We're absolutely sure that, if I can use this metaphor, your country is a little bit ill for now, it's like a flu, maybe, I hope. We think it will be cured in some point in time. We will wait, we will have good medicine for this. We give it step by step; we hope it will be efficient.

Do Not Abandon Hope

So, we do not lose hope, and we try to build a positive agenda. We still are very much keen on multilateralism. You will hear a lot of opinions in the coming weeks, when we have high-level week in the General Assembly of the United Nations. Not all of them will be coinciding in their messages, but I hope that most of them will be quite friendly, quite open, and in favor of multilateralism, in favor of friendship among people, and economic partnership. I think it will be for the benefit of those who follow us, of future generations, and that's what we are keen to do, no matter how difficult it may seem.

And with your help, of course, I think we will move forward. Let's not lose hope. Let's hope for the better! I wish all of you good luck, success. Thank you. [applause]

I'm sorry I am not able to take any questions this time, but I really have to rush to another meeting. And the traffic is terrible in New York City, especially in this part, so I need to rush. Thank you very much.

ROGER STONE

It's a Fight for the Republic, Not the Two-Party Duopoly

This is an edited transcript of Roger Stone's live-streamed video address to the Schiller Institute Conference on Sept. 13, 2018. Stone is a longtime friend of President Donald Trump and a legendary political operative, who was a key mover in the 2016 victory of Donald Trump.

Thank you very much. First of all, I guess I should say that I'm delighted that this worked out logistically so that I was able to join you. I think it's very important to say at the top, that the work that the international Schiller Institute is doing for both peace and prosperity around the world is very important work. I first became acquainted with Dr. Lyndon LaRouche back in 1979 when he was

Schiller Institute

Roger Stone

a candidate for the Democratic nomination for President and played a very important backstage role in the election of our last outsider President, Ronald Reagan.

I have great admiration for Helga Zepp-LaRouche, who is with you today. I think these people are doing an extraordinary job to try to forge greater understanding of the international issues that would bring my country—the United States—and Russia, China, and virtually every country on the globe into some kind of harmony, so that we can all live in both peace and prosperity. So, I salute you for being there today and participating in this conference.

I have been a friend of Donald Trump for 40 years. I

President Trump speaks to hundreds of autoworkers at the American Center for Mobility in Ypsilanti, Michigan, March 15, 2017.

first thought of the idea of Donald Trump as a plausible and viable Presidential candidate in 1988. I thought of this because I saw he had the courage and the determination, and frankly the fortune and the public recognition, to be a viable candidate. But also, that he was not beholden to any of the special interests, any of the neo-con elements that have driven the United States into the ground, into 30, almost 40 years of unprecedented decline.

I tried to get Donald Trump to run again in 2000. I wanted him to challenge both the Republicans and the Democrats. But he correctly determined then that probably one needed to be either a Republican or a Democrat to be elected President, because of the structural prohibitions to an independent candidacy. Namely, it's difficult to get on the ballot; it's impossible to get into the national debates, and so on.

By 2012, I think he was ready, but the country was not quite ready; meaning, I believe, that the United States had to suffer all eight years of decline under Barack Obama and his globalist policies before they were ready to entertain the idea of a President who had never held public office, who had never been a governor or a senator or a general in the military, which may be the most political job of all. But America was ready.

False-Flag Attack Aimed at Trump

What I have seen in this administration is very similar to what I saw in the administration of Ronald Reagan, who I worked for in the 1976, 1980, and 1984 campaigns for President. When the political establishment, when the two-party duopoly, when the globalists that we call the neo-cons cannot defeat you, they seek to co-opt you; they seek to surround you. Here's how

the argument goes: "Well, Mr. President, we know how all of this works. We're experienced in government. Let us help you here." Of course, they aren't interested in helping the President, they're interested in deluding or derailing his policies.

Case in point, sadly, is the situation in Syria. How ironic that right after Donald Trump woke up one morning and tweeted that it was time to get our troops out of Syria, that Assad attacked his own people with a chemical weapons gas attack. Or did he?

Any reasonable person who understands geopolitics, understands that people don't do things that aren't in their interest, leaders don't do things that aren't in their interest. Assad not only had the upper hand against the rebels, but we know that Assad entered into an agreement with the Russians, certified by Secretary of State John Kerry, who said he had no chemical weapons. We also know that Assad is a canny enough politician to understand that the world community would condemn him across the board for the gassing of his own people; which is why he didn't do it! It was most likely a false-flag operation. How many times can they pull the same stunt? This is now twice, and they're probably warming up for the third attempt to use this false-flag technique.

Sadly, the President has surrounded himself with a number of advisors who did not vote for him, did not support his candidacy, do not support his reform agenda either on the economic front or the domestic front, or on the foreign policy front for that matter, and are committed to nothing less than his removal. It is extraordinary that despite these advisors, he has cashed in the Iran nuclear deal which was most likely, in my opinion, a fraud to begin with. One has to wonder, why aren't all the terms of the deal in the document that was shown to the American people? What are all these side deals with hundreds of millions of dollars, literally pallets of American cash, going into the pockets of Iranian politicians? Why weren't the American people told about any of that?

In addition, you have the President's economic record. Many of you may remember, under Barack Obama we were told that anything in excess of 2% GDP growth was just structurally impossible; couldn't be done; you don't understand the new world economy. America's greatest days are behind us! We just need to recognize we're no longer a world leader. Just get prepared to cinch your belt and accept less.

Well, Donald Trump doesn't believe that. In fact, Donald Trump's greatest sin in the eyes of the two-party political establishment is his commitment to American exceptionalism; his patriotism; his belief in American sovereignty; and his strong desire for peace. Better relations with the Russians and, if they will come to the table, the Chinese. Oh my God! He's a peacemaker! We haven't had one of those since, oh I don't know, Richard Milhous Nixon, a man who reached a Strategic Arms Limitation with the Soviets, a man who opened the door to China, a man who ended the Vietnam War on a much faster timetable than the Pentagon that probably didn't want to end it at all.

Stay Out of Woodward's Gutter

It's kind of ironic that Bob Woodward is back in the news. Here's a man who lied about being a military intelligence briefer for the Nixon White House; lied about his relationship as a briefer for General Alexander Haig, the White House Chief of Staff; lied about Deep Throat—there is no Deep Throat, folks. It's most certainly not Mark Felt, the FBI agent who was in a position to know none of the information that Woodward and Bernstein said was passed on by their source. But the same Bob Woodward who lied about Iran-Contra, lied about President Ronald Reagan.

This is the man who said that he gained access to

Special Counsel Robert Mueller.

former CIA Director Bill Casey's room and conducted an interview in which Casey confessed everything. The problem with that is that Casey had been felled by a stroke, and according to his doctor, his wife, and his daughter—both of whom are friends of mine—he had lost the capacity for speech. So, how could such an interview take place? Simple. It didn't. Now, you have the same phenomena where Woodward is lying about this President.

Where I'm disappointed, and I say this candidly to you, is that the President shouldn't get down in the gutter with the *New York Times*. He shouldn't get down in the gutter with Bob Woodward. I can tell you exactly who wrote the famous anonymous *New York Times* op-ed right here today. This is breaking news. You know who wrote it? No one! It's a fraud! It's a fraud upon the people. It's a MacGuffin, it's a device designed to undermine the President.

Moving on to Robert Mueller

Now let me say, before we move to some questions that you have about Robert Mueller—ironically, the man who penalized Lyndon LaRouche as part of the prosecution team in Boston—that tried to silence that great world patriot who is now on a mission, despite the fact that Mueller can find no Russian collusion with the Trump campaign. "Collusion" is defined as coordination, conspiracy, working in concert. That never happened. Yeah, we have evidence of Russian meddling in our election. Do we think that we in the United States have not meddled in foreign elections, specifically in Russia? Who do you think financed the election of Boris Yeltsin? Why, that would be Uncle Sam. Were we interfering in the most recent Israeli elections? You bet your ass! That's what we do.

But now we act like this low-level, ham-handed, ineffective Russian meddling, most likely done by people who have English as a second language based on their social media output, which had no effect whatsoever on the election, is being held up as proof of the success of

Mueller's probe. Also troubling is the unconstitutionality of Mr. Mueller's appointment.

You see, Mr. Mueller has not been confirmed by the U.S. Senate; there is no Federal law in place that holds for the creation of his position. He has unlimited budget; he can take on as many hungry left-wing prosecutors as he wants. It's amazing that virtually none of them—in fact *none* of them—are Republicans. What are the chances of that? Yet we're told by the courts, at least so far, that his appointment is perfectly proper because he is being overseen by an elected official, Donald Trump, and an appointed official, Rod Rosenstein, who was appointed by an elected official, and confirmed by the Senate. The problem with that is that both Mr. Trump and Mr. Rosenstein are at a minimum witnesses, and more likely subjects of the very investigation of which Mr. Mueller is engaged.

After all, it was Mr. Rosenstein who got caught red-handed writing a memo to the President telling him how and why to fire FBI Director James Comey. That came as quite a surprise to Comey, because he thought Rosenstein was one of his closest friends. Rosenstein is mortified because he thought he could do this weasel act behind the scenes, and he would never be outed. So, his consolation prize for the Deep State was the appointment of Robert Mueller.

Mueller is an interesting fellow. He is the man who covered up Saudi involvement in the 9/11 attack on the United States. There were no less than 16 reports from the Florida Department of Law Enforcement—that's our state police—about strange men who were training at a Sarasota, Florida-based flight school. Mr. Mueller failed to investigate those tips, but then, after the fact, investigated a local Sarasota-area Saudi family that was harboring these men in their home. These Saudis had disappeared in the dark of night, leaving behind all their personal effects: their cars, their clothing, their jewelry. And Mr. Mueller certified to the Congress and to the people of the United States that there were no ties between that Saudi family and the 9/11 plot. We now know that that was a lie. Freedom of Information Act-acquired documents from the Federal government prove it.

But then again, it was Mr. Mueller who let four men rot in a Boston jail, who he had convicted of murders that he knew they didn't commit, solely because it would have exposed Mafia FBI informants in the Whitey Bulger case. Then there was the anthrax scandal. Mueller arrested the wrong three men. The man he did ultimately arrest amazingly died in captivity within 24 hours of a Tylenol overdose. Then of course, there's Mr. Mueller's role in BCCI or Lockerbie Flight 103. We can go through the list. He is the cover-up artist for the Deep State.

They say, "Oh, but Mueller's a registered Republican." Try not to think of American politics anymore in terms of Republicans and Democrats; it's an outdated way of thinking. This is a contest between outsiders and insiders. Mr. Mueller has been the hit man for both the Bushes and the Clintons. He is the Lord High Executioner for the Deep State.

What will happen here? Where will this all go? Well, he plays by no rules, so the wide supposition that he would wrap up his investigation by Election Day or by September 11, or by the end of the year, I think that is wishful thinking. He is determined to remove President Donald Trump from office on any thin reed necessary. If the Democrats are successful in winning control of the U.S. House of Representatives, there will be a vote of impeachment. But for students of American government, our Constitution, impeachment is not removal. Removal from office requires a trial and conviction in the Senate to remove this President. That requires two-thirds of the votes of the U.S. Senate; unlikely while we are having an economic boom that is only going to get stronger with each passing day.

I myself have been subject to the inexorable inquisition by this Torquemada, who has—and some of you may know—interrogated as many as twelve of my current or former associates, dragged as many as eight of my current or former associates before the grand jury. This I can tell you with every confidence: he can find no evidence of Russian collusion; he can find no evidence of Wikileaks collaboration; he can find no evidence that I knew about the acquisition and publication of John Podesta's devastatingly embarrassing and incriminating emails. I will confess to two things. I might as well say it right here, so you know it. I do like Russian vodka, so arrest me.

Let me say in conclusion, that it has been a pleasure to be here with you today. I would be happy to take some questions and participate as the program goes forward. Thank you very much for your kind invitation.

President Donald Trump and Coordinated Belt & Road Investments

This is an edited transcript of the exchange between Roger Stone and Helga Zepp-LaRouche following Mr. Stone's presentation.

Helga Zepp-LaRouche: Hello Roger, I'm happy that you are able to talk to us, because you are one of the more fun people of America. [laughter]

But, I really do think that Willy Wimmer, the former Deputy Defense Minister of Germany during the Kohl Chancellorship, is right—that the only thing standing between all of us and World War III is Donald Trump. I think that, unfortunately, is correct.

But in light of this, I think it's very unfortunate that President Trump's relationship with Xi Jinping—which I think is still existing and very good—but with the tariffs, the Chinese are now extremely upset, and feel that this is what could become a trade war. Prime Minister Li Keqiang has said repeatedly that there is a better way to balance the trade deficit, by increasing the size of the cake: If the United States would agree to collaborate with the Belt and Road in third countries, like Latin America, Asia, Africa, even some European countries, there could be joint investments, so by increasing investments, you would balance the trade.

I think that would be more profitable, because I think some of the tariffs also hurt American consumers, because of the increased prices. And some American corporations have also explained that they're not happy, because it also hurts American firms.

Do you see any way to correct policy in the direction I'm suggesting? There is a tremendous opportunity right now. The Forum on China-African Cooperation summit in Beijing consolidated an enhanced and much deeper relationship between all of Africa and China.

The Chinese have repeatedly invited the United States to co-invest together. There are so many projects which are vital for the future of all of these countries.

So, my question is, do you agree with this approach, and what can we do to help to move things in this direction?

Roger Stone: I do agree with that approach. First of all, I must tell you, I don't think Donald Trump is a big fan of tariffs. I think he used them as a tool, as a tactic to get the attention of the people he wants to negotiate with, and to bring them to the table. The President has said repeatedly that he's a free trader, and I think he is. But he wants *fair* trade, reciprocal trade. How about a trade agreement that benefits both countries, as opposed to the NAFTA agreement, for example, that seems to benefit our trading partners, but not benefit us?

The Chinese, I think, had a major impact on the President when they visited Mar-a-Lago in Palm Beach, Florida and I think that the personal diplomacy is the way to break through. The only way the President can get around his own deep-state advisors, is at the urgent request of the Chinese. From the President's point of view, he could say, "Well, the tariffs worked. They got the attention of the Chinese, who have been taking advantage of us in some areas."—and they have. "They're ready to come back to the table! So, I've achieved my goal."

Recognize that the President's trade policies and his imposition of tariffs in some cases, is to negate old trade agreements which seem to fit in this "one size fits all" multinational bastion, as opposed to sitting down with individual countries—the U.K., France, Germany, China, Russia—and negotiating individual deals that speak to the strengths and weaknesses of those individual countries and our own country. That's a far more intelligent approach than this one size fits all, sign here, 300-nations trade deal, which just hasn't served our country very well.

When the President met with the Chinese in Palm Beach, they asked for the extradition of a Chinese national who is seeking asylum in the United States; the President promised to hand the man over. He is not wanted for crimes in the United States, he is wanted for crimes in China. Yet the President's own State Department and his own Justice Department have stalled what is very important to the Chinese, but frankly unimportant, at least on the surface, to our country. And that—believe it or not—is a sticking point, so much so that the Chinese went to Dr. Henry Kissinger and asked him to send word to the President that this was important to them! And meaningless to us.

Yet, there has been no effort, to date, to send that Chinese national back to face justice in his own country, where he's wanted for mega-cyber-financial crimes. What business is it of ours?

So, I'm still hopeful that you can have even a Big Three, even a Big Four summit, where we could make substantial progress on these issues. We would be much better, from the point of view of world prosperity, and the prosperity of our own country, working with China, working with Russia, as opposed to having a new trade war.

I'd be happy to take another question. Thank you, Helga. That was a good one.

HELGA ZEPP-LAROUCHE

Be Passionate to Save Humanity Now— At this Historical *Punctum Saliens*

The closing remarks for the New York City Conference of Schiller Institute founder Helga Zepp-LaRouche, on Sept. 13, 2018.

I think America will probably decide the outcome of this present historical fight. If the United States were to go under, which it could,— Because if these economic reforms proposed by my husband are not adopted, I think the danger of a collapse of the system will really become more and more evident.

Unfortunately Roger Stone had to leave. I think that there are certain parameters that show that the United States is not in good shape. Even if Trump has created some jobs—that's very good—there are parameters which are horrible! Look at the fact that life expectancy in the United States, which supposedly has the most powerful economy in the world, has been going down for the last two years, in all age categories. Now, if there is any parameter which tells you if an economy is doing well or not, it's whether life expectancy is increasing or decreasing. That should be a warning sign. Why is this happening? Because of an increase in the death rate—alcoholism, drug overdoses, suicides because of depression. Depression, why? Because if you have no future, then you give up at a certain point.

So there is no reason to think that we are out of trouble. The need for infrastructure could not be more obvious than in this place. The condition of the subways, for example, which Diane Sare reports to us every time there is a fire in the subway or some line goes out—and look at the potholes, the condition of the roads, the rush hour traffic in New Jersey. People become crazy, they drive like madmen. They drive for two hours in the morning, two hours in the evening, sometimes longer—this is not a normal condition.

The fight is to get the United States to join with China and the other countries in the Belt and Road Initiative, and to rebuild the United States. If you have some vacation time, go to China: It's really an important experience. I think some of you were in China last year. Not that everything there is perfect, but if you look at the infrastructure, you go on the fast trains—it is a pleasure! You truly enjoy travelling on these fast train systems. You can go to some of the main stations, they're like palaces—lot s of marble, big, not crowded like here, because it is well organized.

Look at the changing of the entire region from Beijing to Tianjin to Hebei. All the heavy industries are being relocated out of Beijing into Hebei and to a new city. They are building a completely new system whereby everyone should be able to reach their workplace via modern infrastructure within 20 minutes.

George Washington

George Peter Alexander Healy, 1858
John Quincy Adams

Abraham Lincoln

Franklin D. Roosevelt

This is what should be done with New York! You should take the whole region of Philadelphia, New Jersey, and New York, and think about how to plan new infrastructure arteries—new highways, new tunnels, and new fast train systems. You should have a maglev system for intra-city traffic. But first you need to have a clear idea of what you want—then this is clearly what you will influence the Trump Administration to get for the nation. Keep studying; I know many of you went to the Science of Economics classes given by Dennis Speed, Will Wertz and Jason Ross. Keep doing that! Because we need educators who can educate other Americans about true physical economy. That will become more and more important.

John F. Kennedy

The next seven weeks or so until the midterm elections are crucial. Help us spread the message that it *is* a question of war and peace—that Trump be sustained in the Presidency through the midterm elections.

This is really something to be patriotic about. America has a great tradition: The American Revolution—the American War of Independence against the British Empire. America had great presidents—George Washington, John Quincy Adams, Abraham Lincoln, Franklin Roosevelt, and John Kennedy, most prominently. The American System was once a beacon of hope and a temple of liberty for the rest of the world. Get back to that, and I think that the potential for the United States to again become a friend to all countries is there! If the United States were to say that it wants to be part of this new paradigm, there would be no problem at all.

I want you to have this vision. Be happy and get as active as you can. This is not a moment to sit on the fence and look at things. Remember what I said earlier about a *punctum saliens* in history, in which all developments lead to one moment. If we blow ourselves up in nuclear war, which could happen over the Syria crisis, all of what your parents, your grandparents, and all the generations before did, was in vain. All the music Beethoven composed will be lost—maybe saved only in the Voyager, because they put Beethoven's music, and Furtwángler's composition in the Voyager spaceship, which about a year ago left our Solar System. So maybe it will survive only in that way. But frankly, I would appreciate it more if it would be practiced more here. [laughter] I think the New York Schiller Institute Chorus is a very good place through which it should spread.

Everything is at stake. Knowing that, you should be full of passion and help us, and we should all help each other to save this beautiful humanity, because the thought if it vanishing is not acceptable. [applause]

BEIJING FORUM KEYNOTE

China-Philippines Education Forum: Culture, Talents, and Education Under the Belt and Road Initiative

by Butch Valdes

Butch Valdes, founder of the Philippines LaRouche Society, presented the following keynote speech on Sept. 6 in Beijing, at the China-Philippines Education Forum, hosted by the Economic Observer, *a weekly newspaper based in Beijing and Shandong Province. The event was attended by education ministers, students, and businessmen. This is an edited transcript.*

China-Philippines Education Forum

Butch Valdes speaking before the China-Philippines Education Forum in Beijing, China, Sept. 6, 2018.

Greetings! I am honored to have been invited to this forum, organized specifically to foster dialogue between our two nations on the Belt and Road Initiative. I would like to thank the organizers for inviting us to be a part of this significant discussion on the future of mankind.

Today, mankind once again faces a crossroads. One path leads to perpetual war, famine, and disease, while the other leads to cooperation, development, and potentially the greatest cultural renaissance we have known as a species. One path leads to fascism, empire and slavery; the other leads to nation-states and sovereignty of all peoples. One path believes man is created to oppress another, the other believes all men are created equally, capable of noble acts, expressed through universal principles.

Two Views on the Nature of Man

The situation is not new. Throughout history, many philosophers have discussed the nature and purpose of mankind, his relationship with nature, the universe, and to his fellow man.

On one hand, philosophers like Aristotle, Kant, Voltaire, and Nietzsche believed man is merely a higher animal, incapable of noble ideas, and therefore relegated to mere sense-perception, and base instinct.

These thinkers believed that material benefit should be the highest goal of man, and regarded the pursuit of knowledge as a useless endeavor. One of the more contemporary such thinkers, Samuel Huntington, asserted that mankind shall forever be in a state of war, a Clash of Civilizations, because each culture will never find common ground with the other, and conflict is therefore inevitable. Because of this natural state of man, they regard Empire as the highest form of government. If one looks at the 20th Century, it would seem this view of mankind was being played out, through war, famine, and disease. This, they insist, is the natural, ugly order of the universe.

However, there is also an opposite view of the nature of man, one that believes that we were created for a higher purpose, capable of discovering the secrets of the universe, while sharing the discoveries and inventions with each other—that mankind need not oppress each other to advance, but, through Creative Reason, can cooperate for the benefit of everyone.

Schiller Institute

Conference participants at the opening session of the Belt and Road Forum for International Cooperation in Beijing, China, May 14, 2017. Helga Zepp-LaRouche is at lower right.

Whenever mankind has chosen to take this beautiful view of the universe, a scientific, cultural, and economic renaissance soon followed. This group of philosophers includes Plato, Socrates, Gottfried Leibniz, Nicolas of Cusa, and Friedrich Schiller. And, yes, it also includes Confucius and Mencius.

Although living in separate continents, and centuries apart, these great thinkers were as close as could possibly be in their philosophies and intentions for mankind. For Confucius, as with Schiller, the most important was teaching *Love of Mankind* (ren), which Confucius valued higher than life itself. As Confucius says, "All deeds of man must be embodied with it, otherwise they are worthless."

There are many examples of this commonality of ideas found throughout world history. U.S. Founding Father Benjamin Franklin is said to have studied Confucius and was inspired to organize a Republic based on the same kind of principles.

Our own national hero, Dr. José Rizal, had a deep love for the works of the German poet of freedom Friedrich Schiller, which inspired him to write novels illustrating his love for freedom and virtue. Rizal was also an ideological collaborator of Dr. Sun Yat-Sen— both exchanging ideas and aspirations about Nation-hood and development of their peoples.

It is as if there were a bridge of souls linking these great ideas, these great cultures of mankind. These ideas would usher in the most productive eras in human history, as they will today. In the context of mankind's current scientific and technological capabilities, the human race is in the perfect position to make giant leaps once again.

My decades-long involvement with economist Lyndon LaRouche and his wife Helga, have afforded me insight into what they used to call the New Silk Road. Mrs. LaRouche's decades-long involvement in China, organizing for precisely this program (she is known as the Silk Road Lady), has finally borne fruit, and it brings me great joy to see it progressing within my lifetime. Since the early 1980s, the LaRouche organization has been striving to create a philosophical bridge linking all nations and cultures, uniting mankind through great ideas.

Today, there is no greater time for those ideas to come together. Helga LaRouche pointed out that the Confucian tradition is experiencing a great renaissance in China right now, led by President Xi Jinping, who has made it a point that Confucian teaching must be taught on all levels of society. China's direct investments in countries along the Belt and Road have already begun this Renaissance.

African nations, which had been suffering for centuries under the yoke of colonial rule, now dare to dream of industrial development; in South America, much needed jobs are being created, steering those nations away from the drug trade. Even in the United States, China has kept an open-door policy for Americans to enter into mutually beneficial relationships under the umbrella of the Belt and Road; the benefits are clear and measurable.

Because of today's technology, we have listened and learned how China was able to build a new nation out of isolation, how the leadership of China has engaged the Chinese people to participate in the new endeavor, and how China's culture and rich history have been opened to the world.

Throughout its history, the Philippines has been at the center of an exchange of great cultures of both Europe and Asia, West and East. We have long been friends with all nations, through trade and commerce, and culture.

The Philippines and China have had a long and fruitful history of trade and cooperation. Our earliest artifacts reveal the presence of pots and other objects that originated in China, brought to the islands all across the Philippines and Southeast Asia. Since the 1950s, Christian Chinese schools have been operating in the Philippines, recognizing the rich historical bond of both countries. Our most respected businessmen have strong roots in different provinces in China, and some of them have already established businesses there.

Build a Bridge of Souls to Unite All Mankind

It is time to write yet another chapter in the long story of friendship and cooperation, this time under the Belt and Road Initiative, for the benefit and development of mankind.

President Xi Jinping has presented the world a new paradigm for international relations, where all

Attendees at the China-Philippines Education Forum. Butch Valdes is third from right at the front table.

benefit rather than stay subservient; of dialogue not confrontation; of real friendship, not mere alliance. Unlike the forces that seek to destroy humanity through war, famine, and disease, we should seek to uplift all humanity through great projects which lead to greater development. Indeed, as President Xi articulated: Cooperation is a higher principle than competition.

Like all the universal historical figures before him, President Xi's efforts at uniting the world through the Belt and Road, come at a very crucial juncture in human civilization, as those who want to retain hegemony over other nations resort to all means necessary—even nuclear war—to sustain their world order.

But as earlier in history, mankind shall overcome this, and enter into a new World Renaissance, such as history has never seen. The Belt and Road Initiative may be seen as history's offering to mankind, to help rebuild nations, foster new friendships among peoples, and give hope for the future. Let us continue to build that historical Bridge of Souls to unite mankind.

Let us continue to live inspired by the greatest of all possible world cultures and create a permanent Dialogue of Civilizations. Let us be the great people that history has determined us to be today, and for the sake of future generations, work together for a new world renaissance for mankind!

Thank you.

Will U.S. Forces Aid Al-Qaeda in Syria on the Anniversary of 9/11?

This is an edited transcript of an interview with Virginia State Senator Richard Black, conducted by William Wertz on September 11, 2018.

William Wertz: My name is Will Wertz. I am with the LaRouche Political Action Committee. We're here today with State Senator Richard Black from Virginia, an individual who has been quite in the forefront of the fight for justice in the case of Syria and many other countries throughout the world. He has just returned from a six-day trip to Syria.

It is quite important that we're having this interview right now, because we are really on the edge, once again, of another major international crisis. As the Russians and the Syrians have indicated, another false-flag chemical attack is being prepared, this time in Idlib province, in order to encourage the United States, the United Kingdom, and France, in particular, to launch an attack upon the government of President Assad of Syria. This could happen, ironically, in this immediate period on the 17th anniversary of 9/11. The Russian Defense Ministry has indicated today that there was a preparatory meeting in Idlib province, and preparations have now been made for a chemical attack which could come as early as this evening.

So, what we have here is a situ-

Sen. Richard Black

Sen. Richard Black (right) meeting with Syrian President Bashir al-Assad in Damascus, Syria, September 2018.

ation which is extraordinarily dangerous. Senator Black is in a unique position to give us his insights on the situation in Syria. Please tell us about your trip.

Sen. Richard Black: Thank you very much. As you know, I had a military career. I was a colonel in the Pentagon and served in very fierce combat in Vietnam. So I have lived with military foreign policy really throughout my life.

Fake Gas Attack to Trigger Huge 'Reprisal'

My visit to Syria was tremendous. I met for several hours with President Bashar al-Assad, the legitimate, duly-elected President of Syria, recognized by the United Nations as the leader of Syria. This is the second time that I have met with him; I met with him two years ago. This time there was a sort of a buoyancy, a spring in his step, as he sees the final demise of the terrorists who we have funneled into

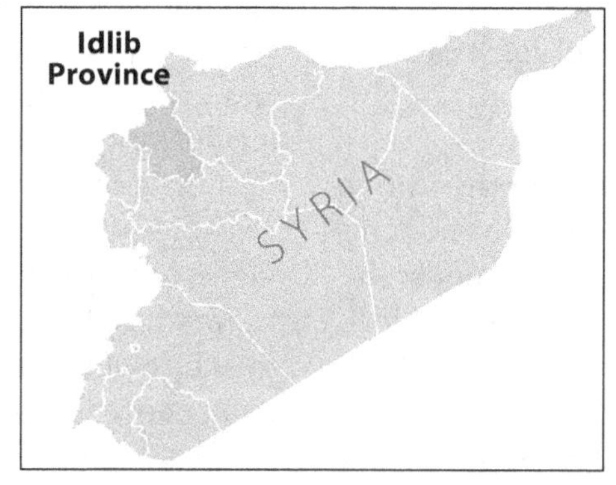

Syria. They're trapped in a pocket, in an area called Idlib province. It's a substantial area, but small in terms of the entire nation of Syria. We have trapped the greatest terror army on Earth, in Idlib province. I say "we"—it's the Syrian army, the Russians, and their allies; but I say "we" in the sense that the civilized world has trapped them. These are the worst of the worst.

The overall commander is a

man named al-Julani. Al-Julani was one of the principal lieutenants of al-Baghdadi, the founder of ISIS. So, al-Julani worked as the head of ISIS in Nineveh province in Iraq. This man is the senior field commander for al-Qaeda in the entire world. And he is trapped along with these other terrorists in Idlib province. The United States, ironically, has a $10 million bounty on his head. All of the rebels have placed themselves under his general command; he is the commander-in-chief of all terrorists in Idlib province. I estimate—no one knows precise figures—but I'm estimating that about 40,000 terrorists are trapped there. They have nowhere to go at this point, because no one wants them.

They're dangerous everywhere that they go. Wherever they go, they are sworn to murder all infidels: all people who are Christians, Jews, Alawites—it doesn't matter what they are, even Sunnis; they are sworn to execute them if they do not adhere to the 18th century doctrines of Wahhabism.

The Syrian army has accumulated troops and surrounded this group; there's a great battle being planned.

The dead-enders of the Western world, the ones who have tried to topple Syria for the last seven years, are determined to the final moment not to give up. We have excellent intelligence out of Idlib province that British MI6 agents, working through a group called Olive, which is sort of a Blackwater spin-off, are planning a gas attack. There is some uncertainty whether it will be an actual gas attack, or whether it will simply be a faked attack like they did in Douma recently, where there was no poison gas used, but was simply a pretence. The idea is to have the White Helmets, a propaganda arm of al-Qaeda, rushing around, "treating" people and photographing. Of course, that's their principal job—to get video. They'll put it out, and they'll say, "Look at this! The Syrians have used poison gas."

Those who have studied intensively, know that there has not been a Syrian government gas attack carried out anytime during the war. You'd never know that from reading the mainstream media, but not one alleged attack has panned out as valid. But the mainstream media will report it immediately. They will not say who did it; they will immediately blame it on the Syrian government, as they have done every time.

It is striking that in all of the years—seven years— not one journalist has ever said, "Can you answer this question? Why, with this vast war underway, would President Assad order the killing of a handful of civilians and never employ poison weapons against the enemy?" There's never been a time that, faced with thousands of enemy troops, that poison gas has been used. I'll give you an example. In the southern part of Syria, there is a hold-out group of ISIS; it's approximately 1,000 individuals. They have a tremendous defensive position; it's very hard to eliminate them from it. It's in the desert, but very hard, and the Syrian army is working, little by little, to try to eliminate this pocket.

If they wanted to use poison gas, the President could say, "Just put it to an end. Let's drop a half a dozen sarin gas bombs. We'll wipe out those 1,000 people and move on." He doesn't; Assad has never authorized the release of poison gas. In fact, there is very little evidence to support the idea that Syria has any poison gas, because under the agreement with the Russians and the United States, they eliminated all of their gas supplies. If we ever suspected that they had it in a building, the United Nations could have immediately had access to it and find it.

Liberate Idlib Province!

So, we know that they are planning a fake gas attack. The irony is that if the U.S. coalition responds by attacking Syria, we will be fighting shoulder-to-shoulder with al-Qaeda—the same group that attacked the Pentagon and collapsed the Twin Towers in New York City, killing 3,000 Americans, causing them to die in a blazing inferno. Will we become their allies? As you mentioned, we are on the eve of the anniversary of 9/11. How ironic it will be if, after these years, we are allied and are fighting on behalf of the very people who carried out the greatest attack on American soil in the history of the United States.

Wertz: I think that's really the most powerful irony in this whole situation. One would hope that the United States would pull back from participation in any kind of military attack on the Damascus government and the people of Syria. To your point, I just read that the monthly newsletter of the Organization for the Prohibition of Chemical Weapons (OPCW) confirmed once again, that all of the chemical weapons in Syria were destroyed or removed. Secondly, as the Russians pointed out, if the United States has intelligence as to chemical preparations being made by the Syrian government to be used in Idlib province, why not give that information to the OPCW, so they can go and inspect? Those are two very direct things that come to mind in this situation.

Black: Yes. Sure. One other thing. In addition to trying to defend the terrorists by the use of this false gas

Sen. Richard Black meets with Syrian Christian clergy.

claim, another angle is to say, "It's just terrible there will be all this bloodshed of civilians, so we shouldn't attack al-Qaeda because we want to spare the civilians." It is the obligation of the Syrian government to liberate Idlib province, and to liberate the civilians. People don't realize the utter cruelty and barbaric nature of these terrorists.

One of the things that the Syrian Parliament is wrestling with right now, is that there are tens of thousands of Syrian women who have been captured and impregnated by these filthy, unwashed barbarians that we have recruited from around the world to topple their government. These are not marriages, these are not families like you think of in America; these are women who are slaves, who have been purchased. They have been kidnapped in many cases.

Many times, particularly with the Christian villages, they will make up lists of the women in the town, and before the battle, they tell each of the soldiers, "If we capture this area, you will own these women. We'll behead the husband, we'll behead the sons of the husband. Then you will possess these women." So, the people calling on us to simply leave them alone, are saying, leave those women to be perpetually raped by these fiends who control this area. I think that would be sinful, it would be deeply immoral in every respect, and contrary to American values.

Role of MI6, Olive, the White Helmets

Wertz: You mentioned earlier the role of MI6 and this company—Olive—which is basically a private mercenary company. It has about 5,000 employees currently and is expanding. They have reportedly been in-

volved in the Idlib operation. And then you also mentioned the White Helmets, who are also set up by the British. So, you have the British directly involved in this provocation in Idlib province, as they have been elsewhere. We did an interview back in April over the Douma chemical attack. The OPCW did not confirm the use of chemical weapons by the Syrian government.

Black: No, they didn't. It was claimed to be a sarin gas attack. One of the unique things about sarin gas is that it's extraordinarily persistent. A sarin gas release site can be detected 30 years later; it doesn't break down like some chemicals do. So, the OPCW went in, and they said, no sarin gas. They did find a group of about 35 people who were dead, but their bodies were staged. I don't think they ever figured out what killed them. But they said it could not have been chlorine gas either, because chlorine doesn't kill you instantly like sarin gas does. Typically, people flee an area infused with chlorine gas, and they might die later on, but they would certainly not be found where the chlorine was.

Interestingly, when the inspectors viewed the bodies and then went back and saw these 35 bodies again, they discovered that some of them had been rearranged, and placed differently during the time that they [the OPCW inspectors] were not there; and that also their gold jewelry had been removed. So, they were murdered, perhaps poisoned, but it was neither by sarin gas, nor by chlorine gas, and I think that was the determination of the OPCW.

Wertz: So here you have the most recent incident which resulted in air attacks, "in retaliation," and the OPCW concluded that chemical weapons were not used.

There is the other irony, which is that British intelligence is directly involved in promoting this thing—the same British intelligence that has been trying to carry out a coup d'état against the President of the United States, which has so far limited his freedom of action to conduct foreign policy. What do you think are the prospects for President Trump being able to pull back from such an attack, if this new provocation goes forward?

Black: I'm a supporter of President Trump. I know some people are, some people aren't—I happen to be. I think domestically he's accomplished a tremendous amount. But when he started off, he put Gen. Michael Flynn in as his National Security Advisor, which really is the closest person to the President. The deep state focussed on Michael Flynn; they knew that they had to get rid of him, because he wanted to diminish tensions with Russia; he wanted to work with Syria and end the war; and they knew that they had a great deal at stake. And so, he was the first that they eliminated.

Michael Flynn and I had exchanged texts back and forth. I don't want to overstate it; I wasn't a confidant of his. But in his final transmission, he was convinced that I had a place working with the White House. He said, "You and I have to meet within the next week." It was during that week that he was swept out of office, and now we have John Bolton.

I will tell you, if someone were to put together one hundred names of foreign policy experts and were to say, "choose the top one," I would say, "Well, I'm not sure that I can do that, but I will pick the bottom one." The absolute worst possible person to control foreign policy, that would be John Bolton. John Bolton is a man of war, of bloodshed, of conflict. And I wish that President Trump would bring back "The Apprentice" [reality TV show] and call in John Bolton and say, "You're fired!"

Trump might do something similar with Nikki Haley, who's our Ambassador to the United Nations. An ambassador is someone who is supposed to find common ground, find ways that nations can work together. Every time she speaks out, she's threatening somebody with bomb strikes, and sanctions, and punishments of different sorts. I think she is a terrible example.

The problem is, the President is not a foreign policy expert. And so, when he sits down with the National Security Council, he's surrounded by these deep state actors, and he may argue against them, he may say, "I want to get out of Syria. I want to do it very quickly." And then, all of a sudden, he has six or eight or ten people saying, "Oh, that would be a huge mistake and here's the reason why." At a certain point, he probably thinks, "I don't want to do something that is going to be disastrous, so I better listen to my advisors."

Trump tried to get us out of Afghanistan, and they were just adamant, saying we can't leave Afghanistan. We continue bleeding lives and bleeding the Treasury of the United States in Afghanistan, with nothing to show for it after 17 years of war. The Taliban are on the march; it's only a question of time before Afghanistan falls.

President Trump unfortunately lacks voices that are close to him, who will raise the other side of the issue, to say, "Mr. President, I disagree. I see things this way." So that if his inclination is towards peace, he can say, "I think I'm going to go with this advisor." That would be a healthier environment.

And so, it's very difficult. I don't know whether Trump can stop an attack based on White Helmets propaganda and a false gas attack—I just don't know.

Wertz: Well, hopefully the preemptive moves by Russia and Syria, in bringing this to the UN and the OPCW—and also, we have been very active in getting the word out, at the UN, in Washington, D.C., and elsewhere around the country—will be sufficient to avoid a disaster.

I would like to ask more about your visit, to Syria. Essentially, you said there was a spring in the step of President Assad, and you probably had an opportunity to get a sense of the way the people of Syria view him. You also mentioned the process of reconciliation that is going on in Syria. So, the question is, how has that contributed toward, hopefully, a resolution of this conflict?

My Two Visits to Syria Compared

Black: You know, I travelled all around the country. When I last visited Syria two years ago, we were in a 12-vehicle convoy with three technical vehicles that mounted automatic cannon; we had attack helicopters, we had a MiG jet flying air support—all of that security to move me from Palmyra to Homs.

This time, however, my security was light. Behind me was a vehicle with four photographers. I don't think they had a weapon among them in their group! I did have a little bit of security, but very light. I wasn't even in a bullet-proof vehicle this time, as we drove across Syria for five hours. We had to use rest stops, and we'd just pick a little—like a shepherd's hut—and we'd go in and ask if we could use their restroom. It was amazing! The spirit of the people is so uplifted, now that they see the terrorists have been driven out of the country: They're hopeful.

It was remarkable. We didn't talk politics with them, we were just friendly. But they would almost invariably speak up and they would say, "We are so grateful for our President and for our army for liberating us and for freeing us from the terrorists." These were common people, these were shepherds, these were people who tend olive groves with little olive trees in the desert. They were in very remote places, almost out of control of the government; and there's this great feeling of optimism.

You mentioned reconciliation. I will tell you, early in

Sen. Black with Soviet-era BMP-1 amphibious tracked fighting vehicle destroyed by Syrian troops, September 2018.

the war, the government set up a Bureau of Reconciliation, where they would allow a rebel group to come over, to return to the government side, and their men had to join the Syrian Army, because Syria has a draft—just like we had, so you can't have draft dodgers; we didn't allow draft dodgers during the Vietnam War. I was very skeptical. I felt, you know, the terrorists, the rebels, they're going to simply say, "Oh yeah, we'll do this," and as soon as Syria's back was turned, they'd stab them in the back and betray them. It just shows that foreigners can never completely understand the culture of another nation, but President Assad believed that this policy would work.

I've spoken to many people, at many levels, and they all agree, it's been a magnificent success. In fact, the soldiers who were recruited from these towns and villages, that reconciled with the government, have joined the Army, and they have fought quite credibly; they've been excellent fighters, fighting against the terrorists. And in exchange, Syria restores their complete civil rights, gives them amnesty—with the exception of a few horrific war criminals—the typical person who got out there and fought the Syrian army, they're given amnesty and restored. And it has worked everywhere, and it has brought unity to the country and peace to the country everywhere.

There is so much hope and optimism—people are rebuilding! Even though we have essentially a blockage—we call them "sanctions"—but international law says, in wartime you can cut off everything except food and medicine. If you do that, that's a serious war crime. We have circumvented that, and we have cut off food and medicine by making it impossible to exchange currency. There's a rule in law that's very fundamental, that you cannot do indirectly what you're forbidden to do directly: In other words, a woman is forbidden to murder her husband; but she might say, OK, I'll hire somebody and have him kill my husband. She can't do indirectly—she is still guilty of murder if she does that.

The same principle applies in international law. So, we have violated international law with impunity, and it's very cruel. All of the refugees want to pour back into Syria, they want to return to their homes, they want to rebuild; they still require some help. And one of the things that's very insidious, is that the United States and the other funders of the United Nations have prevented the United Nations from giving financial and medical support to refugees who return to Syria. As long as they stay outside, in Lebanon and Turkey and Jordan, then we'll give them benefits; but as soon as they return home, we cut it off. We do this in order to perpetuate this refugee crisis.

In spite of this policy, 300,000 people have already returned to the city of Homs; 200,000 have returned to Aleppo; there are thousands returning to Damascus. President Assad made clear to me: "Look, we have to rebuild this country." Syrians, they're very intelligent, industrious people; very honest people. People will say, "We in Syria, we rebuild with our minds and with our muscles." And you can see it everywhere. There was one place where 5,000 university students had taken a week off, and they were there shoveling rubble from the damage done by the terrorists, taking it off in wheelbarrows and just cleaning things out, and getting it ready for the reconstruction, repainting things. So, there is life all over Syria. Syria has come back to life.

Compare that to what the terrorists did. We used to say, the Free Syrian Army, these are moderate terrorists; I went to Maaloula, to a convent where the Free Syrian Army captured twelve nuns and kept them as human shields. The nuns were eventually recovered by the Syrian army and returned; they now have an orphanage there where they take care of children, many of whom are the children of rape, and many others; their families were simply—because they were Christians or something—they had their heads chopped off and the child had nowhere to go. But the nuns now care for them.

Sen. Black visits an orphanage in Maaloula, September 2018.

They took me through the convent; it's an ancient convent, a beautiful place. The Free Syrian Army came in and stole what they could, and then ancient icons that have been there for 500 and 1,000 years, they burned them, they torched them. Everywhere that they went, they killed Christians. The Christians heroically took to the hills that surround Maaloula and they fought. The Free Syrian Army could never overwhelm the Christians, and finally, President Assad sent the Syrian army in to rescue the Christians. Two hundred soldiers died saving the Christians, and most of them were Muslim; most of them were Sunni Muslims, but they died because there is this bond among Muslim, Christian, Alawi, Druze, Ismaili—all of these people. People don't realize the cohesion of the Syrian nation!

You think of it: Here's a nation of 23 million people, relatively small country. For seven years, they have fought the combined industrial and military might of two-thirds of the world's nations. I went to the Army War College; we studied wars. If anyone had said: "Here's a situation, you've got this small nation and you have all of the great powers of the world arrayed against them, all of the media, all of the financial system, everything, how will they fight?" And I think all of the officers in the class would have said: "It's not worth it, just submit to whatever horrors they're going to impose on you."

But they didn't submit. They fought, and they have won. And unless the United States and the U.K. and France, come in on the side of the al-Qaeda, on the side of terror—unless we align ourselves with terror in this final battle, then this small nation will win. I will tell you, there are two things: One is the superior leadership that they have had. It has been magnificent, it has been brilliant. The other thing is, honestly—you know, I'm very deeply religious—I don't know any conceivable way that they could have survived unless it was the will of God.

So, things over there are looking up. And I really hope, if I go again in two years, I hope that the war is ended, the refugees have returned, and I see building going on everywhere.

Going back to that convent: The nuns gathered together the orphans who crowded around me. I had two sitting on my lap. I have 16 grandchildren, so I love small children. If we can bring peace, these little girls will not be sex slaves for ISIS and al-Qaeda. They will have happy lives; they will live normal lives. If, on the other hand, if we had succeeded in toppling the government, all of the Christian men would have been slaughtered and all the women would have all been slaves—many are slaves today, but *all* would be slaves. The Syrian army and their allies have blocked this from happening, and they have avoided one of the great immoral horrors of humanity. And I think that the civilized world should be very grateful to Syria for what they have accomplished.

Part of the Old Souk (market) in Homs has been restored and is now open for business.

Wertz: Absolutely so. What you're describing as the Syrian policy of reconciliation reminds me of the 1648 Treaty of Westphalia, which ended the Thirty Years' War in Europe. The basic conception there was—and I think it's common to all great religions, it's certainly expressed in Christianity, but it's also expressed in other religions—is the concept of acting to the honor, to the benefit, and to the advantage of the other, which is a principle of love. I think that's the power they are expressing, and it has to be unleashed throughout the world at this point.

And Syria—not from their choosing, was part of an overall offensive, including in Iraq, Libya, Syria, and other nations—to bring the world into a very bad state.

'Topple Seven Mideast Countries in Five Years'

Black: People need to realize that our war in Syria didn't begin as us declaring war on Syria. Gen. Wesley Clark, the Supreme Allied Commander in Europe— he's on video, you can see the excellent quality video on YouTube—and he talks about two visits that he made to the Pentagon right after 9/11. The first visit, he asked, "What's going on?" and the general said, "We're going to attack Iraq." He said, "Why? Did we discover weapons of mass destruction?" The general said, "No." He said, "We've got a powerful military, I guess we're going to use it."

He went back on his second visit; he asked, "Well, are we still attacking Iraq?" The general said, "No, it's worse than that." He took a paper, a top-secret document, he waved it, and says, "I've just gotten orders from the Secretary of Defense that we're going to topple seven Middle Eastern countries in the next five years." And they included Libya, Syria, Yemen, Sudan, but ultimately ending up with Iran. None of these countries had done anything to us! They had never done any action that was hostile to the United States.

That was one thing. And then, in 2006, Ambassador William Roebuck was the Chargé d'Affaires of the U.S. Embassy in Damascus, and he published a document— it runs, 8, 10, 12 pages—very widely disseminated throughout the hierarchy of the U.S. government. In this document, which is available thanks to WikiLeaks, he laid out the principles of how we were going to destabilize and topple the government of Syria.

At the time, Syria had enjoyed 40 years of peace with Israel, it was not at war with any nation; it had no debt, it had a very fine economy, not wealthy, but a good economy. It had the greatest religious freedom and the greatest women's rights of any Arab nation: At that time 51% of Syria's college graduates were women. Women dressed as they wanted, they married whom they wanted, they lived in freedom—they could travel around the world, they didn't need the permission of their caretaker, like they do in Saudi Arabia. And they really were the model for all of the Arab world to emulate, because they were the most modernized, the most advanced in terms of their philosophy and their outlook.

We invaded Libya in order to capture weapons that we could send across the [Turkish] border into Syria, to overthrow the country. And of course, the disaster that we caused in Libya is a thing of history: They have no government after seven years. They are simply in a state of anarchy, where people roam the streets and murder and kill and steal, and there's no one you can go to and say, "I want to report a crime." You can't report a crime! Because there's no government—and we did that to them. We slaughtered people, massively, in Libya.

And we did it to capture their very large arsenal, and send it to Syria, so that there we could continue killing people, and we could install a puppet government, run by al-Qaeda. We were trying to have al-Qaeda take over Syria, despite the fact that they had attacked the United States on 9/11!

Just fantastic—the history needs to be written, because it's almost beyond belief. This is not my country—I was a United States Marine. I was enlisted to begin with; I ended up being a colonel. We used to stand at attention in our underwear at night, every night, and we would be ordered to shout at the top of our voices and sing the Marine Corps Hymn; and there's a phrase that says, "I will fight for right and freedom. And to keep our honor clean, we're proud to claim the title of United States Marine."

Our honor is not clean. The deep state that holds its clutches on America; it has smeared filth on the honor of the United States. I respect the flag of the United States, the State of Virginia, and the Marine Corps flag that are behind me in my office, and I want our honor restored. I demand this back: As a United States Marine, I demand that our honor be cleansed, and I will fight to my dying day to see this happen.

Wertz: Well, I think that that sums up your intention and what needs to be done. And so, I thank you very much.

Black: Thank you very much, Will.

As British War Rhetoric Escalates, the Syrians Mobilize for Victory and Reconstruction

by Odile Mojon and Ulf Sandmark

Odile Mojon is a member of the Schiller Institute in France. Ulf Sandmark is Chairman of the Schiller Institute in Sweden and EIR's Stockholm correspondent. They led the Schiller Institute delegation to Syria.

Sept. 16—As lying allegations saturate the news media in Europe and the United States that the government of Syria is preparing a chemical weapons attack on its own people, a European Schiller Institute delegation has just returned from an extended visit to that nation. Our report of that visit hopefully provides a welcome and compelling dose of truth as to the current situation inside Syria, including the urgent need to complete Syria's war of liberation and defeat the last vestiges of barbaric terrorism which targeted that nation. We want to shine a light on the heroism of the Syrian people, who not only defeated the terrorist assault, but are now reclaiming and rebuilding their cities, towns, and villages.

Our Schiller Institute delegation—as well as other delegations of journalists from India, Russia, China, Japan, Czechia, Spain, and elsewhere—was invited by the Ministry of Tourism to visit the 60th Damascus International Fair taking place September 6-15. The fair was an impressive show of Syrian industrial knowhow, covering the broad spectrum of Syria's industrial capabilities. Many of the participants in the fair reported on the devastating damage that has resulted from the war.

Odile Mojon

Reconstruction is the focus now in Syria. Already next month, the 60th Damascus International Fair will be followed up with the Rebuild Syria Fair. Here Ahmad Al-Madi, Marketing Director of the fair, describes to Ulf Sandmark (right) the great international interest in Syrian reconstruction.

But they also talked about the relocation, rebuilding, and restarting of production that are now going on around the clock. This year, 48 nations participated in this fair, many of them from the old Silk Road nations, bringing Syria back into position as an important hub in the China-led Belt and Road Initiative. Several Syrian government delegations have recently visited China, India, Russia and Iran, and the New Silk Road is now part of Syria's economic policy.

At the fair, Sandmark was invited by one of the main Syrian TV channels to participate in a fifty-minute, on-air discussion on eco-

Ulf Sandmark

The domestically produced equipment used to rebuild the Syrian gas pipeline system was displayed in the Syrian pavillion of the 60th Damascus International Fair.

Ulf Sandmark.

The view northwards from the Aleppo citadel over areas of East Aleppo formerly held by terrorists. Standing houses indicate that the fighting was done on the ground, and only partially supported from the air, which would have flattened the buildings.

nomic policy. Sandmark pointed to the importance of the fair as a celebration of the New Silk Road and told of the work of the Schiller Institute, and Lyndon and Helga LaRouche, in promoting it. The *EIR* Special Report, titled *The New Silk Road Becomes the World Land-Bridge*, in its Arabic translation, was shown to the TV audience.

In the ensuing discussion on the lack of money for reconstruction, Sandmark countered the constant over-emphasis on foreign investments, pointing instead to the use of public credit by, for example, American President Franklin Delano Roosevelt in the reconstruction of South Korea and Germany after World War II, as well as in FDR's own New Deal.

He also pointed to the sovereign right of Syria to protect it's domestic industry and agriculture, as it is urgently needed to reclaim and resettle the territories liberated by the Syrian Arab Army from the terrorists. He emphasized that everyone must respect Syria's need to continue its war economy to protect its own physical productive capacity.

In all, Sandmark delivered two on-air television interviews with the two leading Syrian national stations. In those interviews, he, like Virginia State Senator Richard Black, protested against the threat of British, U.S., and French aggression against Syria, under the pretext of a staged,

fake chemical attack in Idlib province to be blamed on President Assad. Sandmark reported on the international Schiller Institute mobilization, the statements by Helga Zepp-LaRouche, and the call-ins to the White House from all over the United States asking President Trump to fire anyone who is pushing for this new attack against Syria.

Inside Syria

The delegation visited the capital, Damascus, and the cities of Homs, Aleppo and Palmyra. Traveling the roads is now safe. Except for Palmyra, these cities have major areas that have been under government control throughout the war and are fully functioning— busy cities with lots of traffic and people in the streets.

Ulf Sandmark

The terribly damaged old city area of Aleppo, intentionally destroyed by the terrorists, is under reconstruction. Streets have been cleared and repaired.

The delegation gathered at the Damascus Old Town Gate Bab Touma, about to start traveling around Syria with the guide, Professor Mahmoud Aboura (left); Odile Mojon (center), and Ulf Sandmark (right).

The exception is the city of Palmyra, which is almost empty with nowhere to stay or eat. It is still under military supervision and special permission is required to go there. In Damascus, most checkpoints seen last year have been withdrawn, as all terrorist-controlled areas have been recaptured. The city can now breathe again, after living in fear for seven years of random grenade attacks from the terrorists. One of the guides stated that during those seven years, people had lived *de facto* in a prison, fearing leaving their homes.

Once one leaves the inner city, however, and arrives at the outskirts of Damascus, the devastation seen in the newly liberated, former terrorist-controlled areas is shocking. This is also true in large parts of Homs and in Eastern Aleppo. Most houses were terribly damaged. As the houses were not flattened, they clearly had not been bombed by airplanes, but instead were destroyed by ground fighting and by terrorists going door to door, burning shop after shop, all around the houses.

Everywhere the rubble was pushed aside on the bigger streets, and the asphalt repaired. All destroyed military equipment has been removed. Reconstruction is going on in stages.

In the areas liberated within the last one or two years, most houses have ongoing reconstruction of new floors and walls, and lights were seen in some windows. In desert areas many, many villages were depopulated, but some of them have now reached a threshold of infrastructure sufficient for former residents to move back and start working the fields.

The main effort has been to restore the basic infra-

Basic infrastructure is a priority. The refinery in Homs (left), one of three in Syria, is in full production. The power lines have been restored, and are now also exporting electric power to Lebanon.

structure. Damascus now has electric power 24/7, after years of controlled, rolling blackouts. The oil refinery in Homs is back in operation, but still producing enough only for domestic consumption. The big fertilizer plant, also in Homs, is now producing 70 percent of the national demand. Most gas pipelines have been rebuilt, almost entirely using nationally produced equipment. The primary oil pipeline to Homs has clearly not been rebuilt, as the road into the desert was filled by endless lines of oil trucks. Long stretches of new, straight roads were built and covered with asphalt to make this "pipeline on wheels" possible.

Aleppo

The Schiller Institute delegation was brought to Aleppo, Syria's second biggest city and the theater of some of the war's most violent battles. The incredible level of destruction tells a lot about the intensity of the fighting, and while one can assume many houses and buildings will be rebuilt, several of the most precious architectural treasures are now lost forever.

Aleppo is not only Syria's economic capital, populated by three million people, it is also among the oldest cities in the history of human civilization, and has been inhabited without interruption for more than 6,000 years. Its importance is related to its geographical position, located on the trade route linking former Mesopotamia to the Mediterranean Sea. This historical dimension is reflected through the many beautiful monuments in the city, among them several which are on UNESCO's World Heritage list, including the Great Mosque of Damascus, the Al-Madina Souk, and the Citadel.

As of today, the mosque is heavily damaged and its 8th century minaret destroyed. The Al-Madina souk, the world's biggest covered market, dating from the 14th Century, was largely destroyed in September 2012, during the rebel offensive, plus later bombardments and battles. At least 700 shops were obliterated, leaving this beating heart of Aleppo's life empty and deserted.

Aleppo's Citadel, where the governmental forces

Odile Mojon

The Souk (Bazaar) in the Old City of Damascus was fully functioning as shown here, throughout the war. After the terrorists had been eliminated throughout region, most military checkpoints inside in this Souk were withdrawn, to the great relief of shoppers, who no longer risked grenades being thrown in the Souk.

held their positions, also significantly suffered when—notwithstanding other destruction—a tunnel located under it was blown up. Although pro-rebel sources attribute this to the government forces themselves, it is well known that the terrorists' strategy was to use tunnels and sewers as hiding places, from which they could pop out unexpectedly, in order to shoot randomly at passers-by, in a strategy of terror.

The Spiritual Warfare over Palmyra

The next day, our delegation took to the road again, this time in the direction of Palmyra, driving through small agricultural places mainly dedicated to olive groves, many of which now resemble desert landscapes as a result of the war.

After long hours, we finally arrived in the city of Palmyra, here again heavily destroyed. Our first stop was to the museum, a place of desolation, where almost nothing is left after the methodical destruction of the collections. Nonetheless, thanks to the dedication of the museum's personnel, cultural authorities and soldiers, many pieces (although only those which could be transported) had been evacuated to Damascus in time.

It is difficult to add to what has been widely reported and commented on about fate of Palmyra's archeologi-

The ancient Silk Road city of Palmyra was intentionally severely damaged by the terrorists. Here the delegation, accompanied by two soldiers, is inspecting the dynamited amphitheater before restoration, which still demonstrates the former splendor of Palmyra.

cal site. On the spot, we could attest to the absence of any strategic military need or gain to be expected from the staged barbarism which took place there, except for a desire to stir awe and terror. Today the most renowned and prominent parts of the site have either been reduced to dust or are in pieces lying scattered on the ground. Such is the case of the Temple of Bel, the Tetrapylon, the Arch of Triumph, and, to a lesser extent, the amphitheater, among others.

Nonetheless, that carefully targeted destruction provides clues as to what would otherwise appear as sheer arbitrariness. Indeed, they have to be understood not only as a will to erase Syria's memory and cultural heritage, but also as components of a message from the leaders of the Islamic state.

The message is as simple as it is monstrous: "Whoever and whatever does not share our barbaric 'thinking' is to be annihilated." Hence, a profound hatred of beauty and knowledge—which was tragically illustrated by the murder of archaeologist Khaled al-Asaad, the former head of Palmyra's antiquities. After being detained and interrogated for a month by ISIS about the location of treasures from Palmyra, he was executed because he refused to cooperate. The renowned and respected 83-year-old scholar was beheaded in front of dozens of people in a square outside the town's museum. It is said that his body was then taken to Palmyra's archaeological site and hung from one of the Roman columns.

The destruction of the Palmyra archeological site made clear the purpose of the jihadists. The final objective could not, by any means, be reduced to the mere conquest of highly symbolic places or the elimination of enemies. It aimed at killing something more essential for any human being: knowledge, beauty, and everything relating to the spirit—to eliminate that which gives people a sense of purpose in life and identity, through their creative mind, as being part of the universal human family. This bestiality in Syria is even more compelling than similar destruction in other countries, such as what had already happened in Baghdad and Mosul, Iraq.

Why so? Because Syria, being at the crossroads of both the ancient and coming new silk roads, being located at a place receiving the nurturing influence of multiple cultures, is by its very history a vivid example of what membership in the universal human family implies. In this context, one can assume that the rage of destroying memory, culture and faith in the human mind was considered by the terrorists as a crucial strategic aim.

Throughout all of our travels, the delegation guide displayed the strong spirit of the Syrian people to fully defeat the terrorists and put the war behind them. He was Professor Mahmoud Aboura, an archaeologist, one who knows every stone in ancient Palmyra and is experienced in restorations of historical monuments. Although deeply shocked by the devastation, which he himself saw for the first time, he pointed out the immediate steps which he would take to restore the dynamited amphitheater.

Back in Damascus, at a press conference, Minister of Tourism Eng. Beshr Yazji called for support from the international scientific community to restore Palmyra as far as possible. He said the severely damaged ancient columns and buildings of Palmyra will be restored, and next year the Silk Road Cultural Festivals in the ruins of Palmyra will be relaunched. Another big trade fair in Damascus for the reconstruction of Syria, called "Rebuild Syria," is coming up, October 2-6.

Enough Documentation of Genocide Against Yemen: Act Now to Stop the War!

by Elke Fimmen

Sept. 13—While the American and European media are daily publishing fictional horror stories about an imagined, "coming humanitarian crisis of unseen proportions in Idlib, Syria," an actual unspeakable, entirely man-made humanitarian crisis is taking place in Yemen at this very moment.

On September 11, INSAN for Human Rights and Peace in Yemen organized the first of its side events at the 39th session of the United Nations Human Rights Council, which had opened the previous day in Geneva, Switzerland.

The INSAN event, "Human Rights Violations and Crimes against Children in Yemen by the Saudi Coalition," was moderated by Dr. Hassan Fartousi, researcher in International Law at the University of Geneva. Dr. Fartousi presented the full atrocity currently underway against the people of Yemen.

The meeting opened with an absolutely shocking video of happy children, who only minutes later were killed by a Saudi-coalition airstrike on their school bus on Aug. 9, 2018. In that attack, 40 boys, ages six to eleven, were killed while on a school trip; eleven adults also died. The weapon was a laser-guided bomb made by Lockheed Martin, one of many thousands sold to Saudi Arabia as part of billions of dollars of weapons exports. Saudi Arabia is the biggest single customer for the U.S. and British arms industries, and both nations support the Saudi-led coalition, including with refueling and intelligence.

Speakers at the INSAN-sponsored event included Aiman Al-Mansour, the President of INSAN; Abdusalam Aldhahebi, activist of INSAN in Sweden; Elke Fimmen of the German Schiller Institute; and Randi Nord, an independent journalist and founder of Geopolitics Alert/USA, who presented documentation of the U.S. and British aid to Saudi Arabia.

Elke Fimmen

Fimmen opened the panel's presentations with her speech, "Justice for Yemen means Justice for the World," underlining that it was the 9/11 attacks that began the series of disastrous geopolitical regime-change wars that have now brought civilization to the brink of superpower thermonuclear confrontation. She called for full publication of the existing evidence of the Saudi role in 9/11. The Schiller Institute, she said, has worked to bring about a Four-Power alliance for peace through development, and developed the "Felix Yemen" Reconstruction Plan in the context of the New Silk Road dynamic. It is only through such a complete shift in international relations that civilization will have a chance, she stressed. The UN experts' report on the humanitarian situation in Yemen, presented in August 2018, clearly documents that the horrendous situation in Yemen has been brought about as a result of Saudi-coalition airstrikes and blockades. Fimmen called for wide circulation of the report and action on the level of the UN Security Council, to stop this war now.

Aiman Al-Mansour presented more shocking facts about attacks on civilians and the situation of children from the UN experts' report in his speech, "Children under War in Yemen." He contrasted the UN Convention on the Rights of the Child with the present reality in Yemen.

We include here relevant portions of the UN Convention on the Rights of the Child, referenced by Aiman Al-Mansour:

Article 6.1—States Parties recognize that every child has the inherent right to life.

Article 6.2—States Parties shall ensure to the maximum extent possible the survival and development of the child.

Article 23.1—States Parties recognize that a mentally or physically disabled child should enjoy a full and decent life, in conditions which ensure dignity, promote self-reliance and facilitate the child's active participation in the community.

Article 24.1—States Parties recognize the right of the child to the enjoyment of the highest attainable standard of health and to facilities for the treatment of illness and rehabilitation of health. States Parties shall strive to ensure that no child is deprived of his or her right of access to such health care services.

Article 39—States Parties shall take all appropriate measures to promote physical and psychological recovery and social reintegration of a child victim of: any form of neglect, exploitation, or abuse; torture or any other form of cruel, inhuman or degrading treatment or punishment; or armed conflicts. Such recovery and reintegration shall take place in an environment which fosters the health, self-respect and dignity of the child.

Abdusalam Aldhahebi concluded the panel, showing pictures of six Yemeni children, appealing to everybody to realize that we are not talking about numbers when we speak about civilian victims, but about precious individuals, all of whom have their own personal history and their own story—and that every one of these children has a right to life and to a future.

Right before this meeting, Abdusalam Aldhahebi, speaking on behalf of the Iraqi Development Organization (ODI), had the opportunity to deliver a hard-hitting, one minute statement to the ongoing plenary meeting of delegations, the press, and UN representatives, in which he called for swift delivery of the new UN high-level experts' report ("Situation of Human Rights in Yemen, Including Violations and Abuses since September 2014," published August 17, 2018, A/HRC/39/43, available at https://www.ohchr.org/Documents/Countries/YE/A_HRC_39_43_EN.pdf) to the members of the UN Security Council, for the purpose of taking immediate action to stop the war and the genocide caused by the Saudi-led coalition against civilians.

That report, under Section E. "Violations of International Law," states in Section 1. Attacks Affecting Humans:

27: From March 2015 to June 2018, there were at least 16,706 civilian casualties, with 6,475 killed and 10,231 injured in the conflict; however the real figure is likely to be significantly higher.

28: Coalition air strikes have caused most of the documented civilian casualties. In the past three years, such air strikes have hit residential areas, markets, funerals, weddings, detention facilities, civilian boats and even medical facilities...

And, under E. 2. Access restrictions:

52: The harm to the civilian population caused by severely restricting naval imports [by the sea blockades] was foreseeable, given the country's pre-conflict reliance on imports. By November 2017, the international community had repeatedly underscored the effects of the existing restrictions and had warned of the catastrophic effects of the announced closure of all ports. The duration of the restrictions raises additional concerns that systemic damage to the economy is occurring.

53: As of April 2018, nearly 17.8 million people were food insecure and 8.4 million were on the brink of famine. Health-care facilities were not functioning, clean water was less accessible and Yemen was still suffering from the largest outbreak of cholera in recent history...

This report had been acknowledged by the new UN High Commissioner for Human Rights, former Chilean President Michelle Bachelet. In her opening presentation to the council's session, Bachelet announced further investigations and the holding to accountability for war crimes all those who have been so accused by the experts reporting to her office. Bachelet referenced the horrible school bus massacre, and other horrific airstrikes that have left dozens of civilians and children killed and injured in Al Hudaydah. She also called the recent Saudi royal order, which practically provides a blanket pardon to members of the Saudi armed forces for actions taken in Yemen, "very concerning."

Aldhabebi, while endorsing Bachelet's statement, nevertheless insisted that since the crimes have been sufficiently documented over and over again, there should be no further delay in stopping the war now and beginning political peace negotiations, instead of waiting for yet another series of reports and investigations.

It is time for the hypocrisy stop. Those responsible for planning and conducting genocide and those guilty of tolerating it, have to be taken to account! If we do not defend civilization and the sacredness of each human being on this Earth, we will not escape the fate that Yemen is suffering now.

May 8, 2014

EXTENDED REMARKS & FACTS:

Economists Who Were Usually Stupid

by Lyndon H. LaRouche, Jr.

Notably, references made here, must begin with these following, necessarily, multiply extended, prefatory remarks. These are made respecting those matters, which will be shown, below, as having been lodged within what are now, in effect, matters subsumed under a necessarily, somewhat extended history of my own early, formal, education, as follows:

My Extended Education

I was born in Rochester, New Hampshire, on September 8, 1922. My own education since I had left a Rochester school at the age of ten, had moved me into a Lynn, Massachusetts grammar school in 1932. That had scarcely been much of a success, as ordinary matters go. Many among the teachings supplied by the Lynn, Massachusetts schools in my own time there, had often been filled out with the relegation of the subject of mathematics and its derivatives, to what is presently traceable to the then wicked influence of Bertrand Russell. That had been an influence which had been felt approximately world-wide, by the time of the end of World War I.

In my experience, there had been some exceptions to a more general incompetence of education in schools; but, those exceptions had been limited to a relatively few classes from among the total. I came to see this more clearly, in my concluding three years at Lynn English High School, which were, otherwise, virtually a total disaster, as, similarly, my later experience during the nominal university education administered to me in a university in Boston and its vicinity, before and after military service in the U.S.A. and, then, Asia after the close of World War II.

The best feature of any competent report on my educational experience, is, still, today, that it was, frankly, the more disgusting as several years had passed.

The Worst Characteristics

The worst characteristics which had been common to the classes in education, were those in Lynn, Massachusetts, first, and, later, Boston. In both of the two cases, the relevant worst effects were the most disgusting with respect to a practice of a body of teaching which had been based on the defense of Euclidean geometry, and its derived expressions, such as the depraved mathematics which had been premised on those fraudulently adopted presumptions which had taken control over trans-Atlantic education, at the beginning of the Twentieth Century, in place of actual science.

This fraudulent substitution is to be witnessed, still today, since the 1900-dated campaigns of David Hilbert, in France in 1900 A.D., and, slightly later, the outrightly Satanic influence of Britain's Bertrand Russell worldwide: that consolidated the beginning of the early 1920s, ever since, up to the present time.

The relatively worst cases of the post-Nineteenth Century's moral and intellectual degeneration in education, generally still worse presently, have been typical of the destructive force of moral disaster, which is quickly identifiable as "reductionism:" a worsening pathology, which had, then, already permeated the educational systems in both secondary and university-bases. This wicked change had been premised upon merely an essentially linear, actually anti-scientific hoax: virtually, an avowedly mandatory hoax, resting on the farcical teachings which were commonly based on the neo-archaic root of an *a-priori,* Euclidean geometry, and on the related offshoots of a mere arithmetic, not an actually physical science.

This was a mere arithmetic which had been installed as a proposed replacement for actual science, and which has remained as increasingly hegemonic throughout both the Twentieth Century, and also the early Twenty-First this far. Those trends of degeneration in educational and merely allegedly scientific practices, and their effects, have remained relatively hegemonic, although entirely fraudulent, and, also, as systemically opposed, fiercely, to any semblance of an actually physical, modern science.

By my time in life, that particular fraud, of Euclidean geometry, had generally saturated the pores of the system in that High School which I had attended in Lynn, Massachusetts, then, in particular, and continues in an actually worse form presently. That factor, was systemically destructive in its effects on the most among the students there, and was, also, visibly damaging to potentially cognitive powers of the students, more generally.

At Lynn English High School

What had saved me from much of this corruption, in particular, went according to the pro-

EIRNS/Claudio Celani

"Watching the Teachers Enter." Lyndon LaRouche writes about the failures of public education when he was a student, some 80 years ago, but since the death of President Kennedy, the quality of education has declined even more precipitously.

verbially Scottish references to the notion of "all that," as having been the interventions, by competent leading elements of the Lynn, Massachusetts directors for the city's educational system, notably senior official Stephens and the head of the Lynn English High School.

There, I was justly rescued, initially, by the results of my simply taking an "I.Q." test, which proved to me (and relevant others), sufficiently then, to be startlingly clear evidence, initially, against the vicious abuses generally practiced, in particular, in the Eighth Grade of school in which I had been virtually pilloried at that time, by the abuse by some of the faculty of the relevant Junior High School, where I had been subjected to such treatment, prior to the taking of that standard "I.Q." test of the time. It was the result of that test, which had prompted the higher ranks of the Lynn school system, to liberate me from the vicious abuse to which I had been subjected by that so-called Junior High School Eighth Grade.

The resulting evidence shown then, and later, was that I had been an exceptional talent. For that reason, I became, soon, a bit later, once more, the victim of a new source for a virtual intellectual "lynch mob" hostility against me personally, which had included a large ration among some of the faculty of the Lynn English High School at this time. The sponsors of that sort of "pogrom," were those teachers of the type who had preferred that the students not actually think too carefully, but, rather, should simply attempt to repeat what they had been taught by the combined efforts of teachers and by the texts supplied.

Thus, what had happened in the 8th grade experience, appeared, afresh, as widely echoed among the faculty at the Lynn English High School. There were some exceptions to such "popular abuses,"[1] particularly among the better scholars, but the ugliness remained the prevalent truth to be spoken respecting the prevalent practice throughout the general environment, there.

The "I.Q." tests which I had experienced, both in the 8th grade case, and, freshly in the Lynn English High School, had each demonstrated a relatively exceptional, so-called "I.Q.," rating, for which only a relatively very small minority of the students were qualified. Unfortunately, the connections to those abuses to which I had been subjected in the Eighth Grade, were not limited to that school; they had been, essentially, the same stupid abuse which would, and did cross-infect a relatively large ration of even the Lynn English High School faculty (with some notable exceptions), within the Lynn school system. The later, second, "I.Q. test," showed evidence of suggested higher achievement levels, with respect to those which had been measured earlier, for the Eighth Grade affair.

There was, nonetheless, a continuing targeting of students who were, not only even merely, "quicker learners;" but, actually original thinkers, a type which were emphatically not wanted by certain, unfortunately prevalent, malicious clusters, assembled from among the faculties in both Lynn and, later, my experience with relevant Boston university educational programs. Some of the faculty are to be blamed in those cases; but, like, the administration of the Eighth Grade, and the later class-work at the High School levels, they were, generally, intellectual disasters in fact: both for the students, and the effects shown in the shaping of their judgments in later years.

Only in few cases, over the full course of that time, those who stood out as valuable exceptions, especially in the non-mathematical aspects of the education, showed their significant resistance to the more popular follies; but they were, nonetheless, only a relative minority. When the faculties were corrupted in that respect, they had been, for the most part, also, even vicious in protecting their often dubious expressions of appeals to an allegedly "popular opinion" of "those regular guys and girls" who were, generally, more concerned with being considered as "popular," than seeking the merits of their future roles in society.

The results of what I have already referenced here, as the twice-repeated I.Q. testing of me, had seemed to have virtually saved my need to sort out good, or, at the least, merely decency, from the intellectual "lynch-mob" sort of bestiality preponderant in the general educational environment. My "I.Q." testings by the educational departments, had occurred on two most notable, relatively successive occasions; these tests had shown me, as also the relevant officials, exceptionally high qualities of competence in my own performances, as shared among the relatively upper ranks of intellectual development within the student bodies during those times. The most notable effect of this testing, was, for me, the importance of seeking to re-enforce what had been tested as indications of my own, relatively superior notion of truth, generally; this would be con-

---

1. I must admit, that the almost regular, weekly beatings I enjoyed from my mercurially disposed, from "enraged to publicly charming" father, were an aggravating consideration in the process as a whole; but, the one factor only re-enforced the other. The only effective resolution, was to rely on my own stubborn commitment to the notion that only the truth of a matter was a satisfactory resolution.

Capricho 37: "Might not the pupil know more?" Francisco de Goya (1797-98).

tinued by me, as a pattern, as from the close of my secondary education into some dismal university years.[2]

My personal experience on this account was never unique in and of itself. The technically identified practice of talking-down students in public schools into a state of moral confusion, and, similarly, also in universities, has been,

now increasingly, a generally accelerated practice of presently current educational institutions, which was a cause for an increased moral and intellectual degeneracy-rate which has been increasingly acute since the assassinations of President John F. Kennedy and his brother Robert, and since the parallel spread of drug-addiction among soldiers and others during the interval of the U.S. part in the worse than useless Indo-China war, as both President John F. Kennedy and General Douglas MacArthur had forewarned, prior to the assassination of John F. Kennedy, and as during the closely following death of our republic's then greatest living military strategist, Douglas MacArthur.

The alleged, chiefly fraudulent "Case of Lyndon LaRouche," has thus continued to reflect what has recently been the usual quality and effect of what I experienced in the setting of the educational systems, of my own knowledge; but, at the same time, it expressed, more importantly, a characteristically declining intellectual quality of the educational, and functionally related institutions, over the course of the passage of recent decades, a moral and intellectual decline which I had already experienced, since my experience with what I have indicated as educational processes, up through the present time. It is, notably much worse, presently, especially among the adolescents, and younger, than ever before. However, the typical sophistry practiced publicly by typical members of the Congress, for example, shows too much of a similarly regrettable performance in respect to the need for truth expressed in the public interest. The decadence of the standards of judgment by the U.S. Congress, has been the fruit of two leading factors: the declining quality of intellectual competence in the U.S. government itself, especially since the assassinations of President John F. Kennedy and his brother, Robert, coincided with the plunge into a British-directed, important increase of relative stupidity within nearly all categories of the general population since the assassinations of the two Kennedy brothers, and the rise of the politically induced, virtually decorticating "Green" intellectual pestilence, which has been increas-

---

2. Although there had been a useful purpose in the "I.Q." tests, their merit was, nonetheless, a matter of estimated relative accomplishments, according to roughly clear and distinct categories; but, they were otherwise matters of pragmatically useful assortments of relative categories, which served as meaningful notions of a series of categories, not an absolute measure.

ingly prevalent throughout most of the dope-soaked ranks of such increasing rations of the mentally and morally incompetent of the increasing rations of the dope-soaked sector and related, "green" brain-drained, and the increasing ration of the often wobbly-headed sections of the U.S. population presently.

Into My University Years

My own university years, had been, essentially, a morally dismal aspect of public and related education. I have recalled it, as, being often begun on a much lower level of the intention of education, than had been the case in the Lynn, Massachusetts high school system. The education of the particular university life which I had experienced, was predominantly below the quality of the education which I had received, earlier, in the Lynn High School. The passage from the President Franklin Roosevelt/World War II generation, into the post-Roosevelt, relative moral and intellectual degeneracy of the Harry S Truman Administration, was directed, via Wall Street, by the Truman-Churchill-Bertrand Russell "Witch-hunt" trend, a trend which had produced an induced, long-ranging decline in the moral and intellectual qualities of performance of the U.S. population generally, even in virtually all relevant categories, moral categories, most emphatically.[3]

My second experience with that same Boston-area University on which my father had repeatedly insisted, had credible exceptions such as an academic year's study in "the German language for us seeking careers involving chemistry," or a smattering of the principles of chemistry in some of the faculty, or, also the literary skills of a certain Dean of the university, and some intermittent, useful snatches of chemistry

New York State/Library of Congress

LaRouche's wartime service, like that of other veterans, meant that they "were no longer children to be taught; we preferred to be those who selected their destiny as a matter of a maturing personal judgment respecting the necessities for the future." Here, returning troops express their jubilation at returning home, Aug. 6, 1945.

caught between-times. Otherwise, the experience there, was an exposure to a chronic sort of pedagogical disaster which had rather simply reflected the influence of the Twentieth Century's fraudulent, but also decaying dogmas of relying on merely mathematics, rather than actually physical science, while tending, either to avoid all actual science, in favor of eliminating the influence of actual science, or, to craft a mere appearance of a glib showing of some of "the real stuff."

Certainly, not all among the professors and instructors, were actually incompetent; but, from the moment of the death of President Franklin D. Roosevelt, the culture of the United States, was already in precipitous decline under the freshly accelerated pressures from the British empire's increasingly over-reaching control of the post-FDR United States, chiefly, then, under the dictatorship of Winston Churchill and, more importantly, the virtual Satan of almost the entirety of the Twentieth Century, Satan's clearly own Bertrand Russell. Such were the exemplary effects which had fostered the predominant spirit

---

3. I treat this delicate subject, in appropriately selected, later chapters following.

of increasingly decadent sophistries permeating the atmosphere of the institution of education itself; this effect was both the principal source and medium of the practiced intellectual, and also moral corruption, if sometimes, even with a mere taint of competence to "so to speak," lend a mere appearance of the poorly refined coating placed upon the correspondingly disgusting cake. The prevalent rule was, of the customarily and monotonously corrupt, "go along to get along" mentality: a spirit of "sham" which has permeated the life of our institutions, not excluding the U.S. Congress, generally up to about the present time.

Somewhat Later:

During that same period, but following the close of World War II, I had returned to the university which I had suffered through earlier, but I had sometimes enjoyed encounters with some eminently important professional physical scientists, and the like, met from the context of such as the Harvard environment. At that time, I was one among those with whom I had recently returned from the concluding term of my military service in Asia; and, I had enjoyed the degree of confidence which I had brought back with me from the latter phase of that military experience abroad; but, I had also had more than enough of the university to which I had mistakenly returned, briefly, after military service. All-in-all, this was a tasteless experience which I briefly endured only for reason of the pressures from my father. However, his pressure on that subject had lost any further meaning for me as a dweller in the post-war world: I set forth, thence, to seek out, and make my own future, thenceforth. The pathway leading up, was chiefly rugged; but, it was not long before the appropriate remedy appeared; now, I had excelled within the scope of my professional assignments, until the FBI moved in to spoil matters for a time.

Many among us, notably from my own post-war generation, reacted similarly to my own reactions, in the respect, that being "away to wartime service," had marked out an interval of lapsed time between entering and leaving military service. That circumstance, had, thus, tended to separate our pre-war outlook on society, from our post-war sense of personal morale, and morality, alike, from an experience of an adult identity under the resonant leadership of President Franklin Roosevelt.

For me, this resonance was potently emphatic. This effect included my often justly contemptuous attitudes toward the "kid stuff" aspects of university life: we, of many veterans among my generation, were no longer children to be taught; we preferred to be those who selected their destiny as a matter of a maturing personal judgment respecting the necessities for the future. We may have been denied that goal, from case to case at hand, but our intention was for scientific, economic, and cultural progress.[4] In the meantime, under Truman and the continuing "witch-hunt" moods even under President Eisenhower's Presidency, the pressures reflected the heavy hands of the notorious Dulles brothers, as we had known this fact during the course of World War II itself.

The single most notable implication of the aforesaid experience with both secondary, and higher education at the relevant institutions of learning, is that my intellectual achievements in later adult life, as in Lynn, Massachusetts' I.Q. examinations, were, in performance, among those in range of the standard of the 125-148-score level denoted by the relatively different standards of the Academic and Military-service ratings: obviously, merely approaching the "genius" sectors, if not reaching it; but, nonetheless, thus approaching the relatively highest ranking professional competence attained during

---

4. "Old dogs," with whom I might be classed today, tend to have that spirit which I share presently on this account. Some among our generation's sons and daughters are prone to respond to that spirit which resides as if within a resonance somewhere in our bones. The "I.Q." issue associated with my undergraduate and later development, is highly relevant with respect to the two upper strata of the relatively senior generations, much more so than citizens now in their twenties, or their parent's generation. The quality of both those latter, a generation later, have been, generally much poorer in education and in economic and cultural opportunities, than my own immediately junior generation of the approximately fifty-to-seventy-year-old batches, or those presently living still older, if they are still economically and culturally active.

my many later decades of my profession as a physical economist in the domain of real life within our nation and abroad.[5] The actual problem was to be located within the social system of so-called "Popular Opinion."

The Standard for Meeting Achievement

The root of those defects has lain, clearly, within the characteristics of a relatively declining quality of so-called "public opinion," an effect which tends to determine that the younger generations will be, since the end of the 1960s, less intelligent in actual practice, than those of the older. This, somehow, despite the true genius of the founders of modern European (and, hence, also American) intellectual achievements in modern science and Classical artistic performance, who are best gauged, practically, as by the standard of the leadership in the actual founding of all competent modern science, such as that under the leadership of such as the actual, trio of original founders of modern science, in order of sequence: (1) Filippo Brunelleschi; (2) Cardinal Nicholas of Cusa; and, (3) the unique achievement of Johannes Kepler of the original discovering of the existence of the Solar system.

Later, there were the foundations laid by the Winthrops and Mathers of Seventeenth Century Massachusetts, or their successors, such as Cotton Mather, in particular, who fostered the great genius and founder of the American Revolution, Benjamin Franklin, and such singularly great geniuses as our General Alexander Hamilton (the true founder of the economic system of the original U.S. Federal Constitution).

The physical science founded by Brunelleschi, Cusa, and Kepler, situated the progress effected by such outstanding figures, such as the true giants of the Seventeenth and early Eighteenth centuries, as Carl F. Gauss had been followed by his most brilliant student, Bernhard Riemann. Riemann made the revolution in science which the great Max Planck and Albert Einstein had later defined, respectively: the new minimum (Max Planck), the new maximum for science (Albert Einstein); and then, as being the successor for Kepler's earlier role in Renaissance triad: the great Russian-Ukrainian, Vladimir Ivanovich Vernadsky, whose work in the foundations of physical science, had achieved a higher meaning for insight into man's relationship to the Solar system as such, than ever before: the unique, astrophysical efficient principle: the essential function of ontological advances in human life, as a basis for existence within the Solar system (and beyond) *per se.*

Education Since Franklin Roosevelt

Afterwards, the assassinations of President John F. Kennedy and his brother Robert, were combined with the effects of the wretchedly wicked venture into the graveyards of souls, which had even more than destroyed human bodies in the lunacy of the U.S. launching of its War in Indo-China, a war which was merely another holocaust of wasted lives set into motion by the influence of the British empire under the influence of the frankly Satanic Bertrand Russell.

The concomitants of all this, for me, had been, that since the testing which had led to my "double promotion" from the Eighth Grade, I had come to understand, increasingly, on successive points in what was for me, the history of my reflections: the specific failures of the educational processes to which I had been subjected, and which I had sometimes bitterly resisted, as in my public schools' and in the aborted quality of most aspects of university education. This became more, and more clearly understandable as time had passed.

Post-World War II times and their developments since the time of the death of President Franklin D. Roosevelt, confronted me with the essential lesson-in-life: to become fully aware, in retrospect, of my own intellectual vindication

---

5. A "physical economist," is efficiently defined as one devoted to those principles of physical chemistry chosen for purposes of economic practice, rather than the foolish babble of statistical mathematics. Science is a matter of achieving the future realities unknown to the mere past and present, as even the most modest appreciation of the principles of chemistry-as-a-science demands. I have been fairly regarded as, in fact, the most successful U.S. forecaster since the late 1950s. My successful debate against U.S.A. and leading British economics circles of the celebratead December 2, 1971 Queens College debate, has been a convenient marker of reference on this account. See *EIR*, January 18, 2018, page 38.

on precisely that account: an achievement largely embodied in a deepening of a sense of a necessary distance from what had been, chiefly, a past into which I had come to know I had been dumped, in the main.

In fact, it had become, and remains the fact that my intellectual development in respect to these matters of education, had been far above the level of virtually all my known contemporaries, not only in both secondary schools and my later experience of then-customary university indoctrination. That has been the case ever since, as continued through the present time: but that also in the matter of the proper principles of statecraft.

My particular hatred, today, on this account, has been against the mis-teaching of science, a practice which has been premised on the basis of merely mathematics as such, as in the present tradition of David Hilbert and Bertrand Russell. This means that we must, urgently, end the fraud typified, by such cases as the stubborn hoax of Euclidean geometry, which persists, in the guise of Hilbert and Russell, as the most effective instrument of evil against humanity since Zeus and Satan themselves. My sharpest and most bitter insight into the root-cause for my own hatred of that wretched sort of education which I had, largely experienced: it presents a reflection of my confrontations with the post-World War II doctrines of the British Empire's leading professional Satan of the Twentieth Century, the same Bertrand Russell, himself.

My Own Profession

Today, my initial, and still-current profession, has been that of employment as a specialist in economic forecasting, a role which had begun during the late 1940s, and, soon-thereafter, as a secondary executive in the same consulting firm. Those few years in practice in that position, were, first a consultant in the field, and, then, a secondary executive official of the same firm's executive.[6]

Nevertheless, during that lapse of time. I had already become among our nation's leading economic forecasters, in the middle to late 1950s, and since, now, about now sixty years ago, and still presently. My rise to first-rate status in actual achievements in forecasting, had initially spanned an interval of time, from the time of my 1968-1971 forecast of the profound, coming crisis of the U.S. economy, whose result has been, since, a continuing, downward trend in the physical aspects of the U.S. economy, an economy which has continued to plummet since then, up through the present date at the brink of a general "bail-in" collapse of the trans-Atlantic region of the planet.

I attribute my success as traceable, originally, to the impact on me of such as, most notably, originally, that of such as the Gottfried Leibniz, who had been the inspiration for the Eighteenth-century American Revolution, especially under the role of Benjamin Franklin, and the founding of modern economic science as such, by the memory of the British-assassinated, Major-General Alexander Hamilton's systemic perfection of his design for the four founding principles of the U.S. economy, principles which remain as the only actually competent founding principles of a science of

---

6. In fact, this experience had provided me with a solidly successful position in professional economic performance: which had been continued until I had inadvertently crossed swords with the FBI. As was more or less a custom for such encounters, the FBI's wrath produced a divorce from my enraged first wife, a divorce, thus, arranged by an "old family friend," who had assured her, most emphatically, that all of this had nothing to do with the FBI as such. Nevertheless, during the meantime, I had already become our nation's most successful economic forecaster, that beginning the timely outcome of my widely publicized, timely forecast of the probable crisis of the U.S. financial system for within the interval of 1968-71: just in time for the major crisis of 1971-1972. My part in that forecast event had then been prominently featured internationally, in conjunction with a famous defeat of the British spokesman whom I had defeated in a celebrated international conference, held at Queens College, New York City. Nevertheless, during the meantime, I had already become, in fact, among our nation's successful forecasters, from during the middle to late 1950s, already, now sixty years ago, and still presently. My rise to first-rate status on this account, now sixty years ago, had initially spanned an interval of lapsed time, from my 1968-71 forecast of the profound, coming crisis of the U.S. economy which since, then, has been a continuing, downward physical-economic trend in physical aspects of the U.S. economy, an economic trend which has been, since then, continued to the present date, where it hangs at the brink of a threatened "bail-in" collapse for the trans-Atlantic system.

physical economy throughout the entirety of the world of today.

The truth of that success of Hamilton's special genius, has lain within the bounds of the actual distinction of the human species, its distinction as superior to all otherwise presently known expressions of life, as, also, not so incidentally, tied to the greatest chemist of modern life, Russia's greatest modern scientist, Vladimir Ivanovich Vernadsky: the superb scientific genius who had actually discovered the distinctive principle of human life with such remarkable precision, and insight into the meaning of that life within, explicitly, the presently known bounds of the Solar system.[7]

EIRNS

LaRouche attributes his sucess as an economic forecaster to the impact on him of, among others, Gottfried Leibniz, "the inspiration for the American Revolution, especially under the role of Benjamin Franklin," and Alexander Hamilton's American System economics. LaRouche is picture here with this famous "Triple Curve Function," 2003.

I. The Roots of Modern Science As Such

Presently, I continue to trace the actual foundations of modern science back to what is named as "The Golden Renaissance," since no later than the Fourteenth Century. This had been a most profoundly revolutionary turn, upward, into all achievements of modern history, and has been the sources of the actual quality of human mental modern progress typified, by that origin, as by the leading contributions, precisely, in turn, for principle, in the already cited threefold succession of Filippo Brunelleschi *(the physical principle of the ontological minimum)*; Cardinal Nicholas of Cusa *(the physical principle of the ontological maximum)*; and, then, Johannes Kepler, the principal follower of Nicholas of Cusa, thereafter, and of the originally modern discovery of the categorical concept of the existence of the Solar system, as such, by Johannes Kepler.

The triad of the work of those three founders of the original modern European civilization, were coherently related, as founders of all competent modern science. They had lain the foundations for the subsequent genius of such later, exemplary modern geniuses, as Gottfried Leibniz, Carl F. Gauss, Bernhard Riemann, Max Planck, and Albert Einstein. However, from that point in time, on, as during the same time as the work of Planck and Einstein, and times beyond since today, the notion of the very meaning of even the mere name of science, had since been first polluted, and then virtually destroyed: that done, most notably, by those two figures who became prominent for their own specific crimes against science and humanity, alike, since the dates of the period beginning the year A.D. 1900: these were the dates of the foolish figure of David Hilbert in Paris, and, a short time later, Hilbert's frankly Satanic follower, Bertrand Russell.

The common feature of the dogma of both of these latter two cases of Twentieth-century corruption, Hilbert and Russell, had produced a presently continued, generally accelerating, degeneration of the practices of both science and economy, a pollution with the aftereffects reaching (formally) from the onset of the Twentieth Century, to the now increasingly threatened gen-

---

7. The case of the systemic achievements of V.I. Vernadsky is the subject of the concluding chapter of this report.

eral cultural and economic collapse of trans-Atlantic social culture, presently. This has been, a decline which has strictly dominated the United States of America, in particular, since the deaths of, respectively, U.S. Presidents Franklin Delano Roosevelt, and President Roosevelt's implicit echoes, President John F. Kennedy and his brother Robert.[8]

Since the assassinations of President John F. Kennedy and his brother Robert,[9] the economy of the trans-Atlantic region of the planet, has been careening in an, overall, generally downward direction, a continuing process to be located, more narrowly, in the 1968-1971 turnabout into a generally downward, now continuing physical collapse of the immediately trans-Atlantic economies, *per capita*. All allegedly subsequent, actually net economic growth of the United States has fallen, in net effect, as a presently accelerating rate of downward-turning, and still accelerating downward, physical-economic trend, since that time, up to the present date, and, still being extended, prospectively, into the immediate future beyond. This has been, and presently remains a condition immediately threatening a prevalently accelerating collapse-rate of the U.S. economy, which has been accelerated, economically and morally, alike, at increasing speeds of collapse since the succession of the "Junior Bush"-Dick Cheney Administration, and Obama's willful collapsing of the U.S. human economy, all done under an actually British imperial dictatorship over the United States, and our plunging Presidencies, our Congress in the main, all that plunging downward, at accelerating rates, most emphatically, since the close of the William Clinton Presidency, through to this present moment.

---

8. The period of transition, into the modern crisis of the Twentieth though the Twenty-first centuries, so far, had actually occurred during the last decade of the Nineteenth Century. It had been the British Royal Family's ouster of Germany's Chancellor Otto von Bismarck, soon followed by the assassination of France's President Carnot, which had been the opening of the transition to a permanent state of global warfare (with temporary vacations) from the ouster of Bismarck, through to the present state of thermonuclearly threatened world-wide thermonuclear warfare.

9. And, also, implicitly, the related, attempted assassination of President Ronald Reagan. Most of the assassinations of U.S. Presidents, and similar notables, have been effectively identified as having been traced to British Empire operations. Not coincidentally, the victims were usually from among the best Presidents, or Presidential candidates, as I have pointed out crucially significant cases of such coincidences. I have compiled a relevant review of the entire roster of our Presidents, heretofore, with relevant evidence as to correlatives.

The Continuing Downward Trend in U.S. Society

How far beyond will this downward plunge now go?

That will depend upon the arrival of appropriate measures for any possible recovery of the trans-Atlantic economy. That means, in turn: that, at this moment, the probable survival of both peace and the U.S.A. alike, depends on the urgently required, immediate expulsion, for much urgently justified cause, of President Barack Obama. Although the U.S. Presidency, must, nonetheless keep Obama safely alive, even if in the prison which he deserves for his crimes, the security of the United States, and avoidance of thermonuclear warfare, requires that he had been placed, safely, out of the harm's way of both the U.S. Presidency, and that the U.S. citizens of the present and future, would never make the present kind of the same mistake, or its likeness, ever again.

I have recently set forth, in earlier publications, the most indispensable of those U.S. political-economic reforms, which, in particular, should be sufficient to bring about a sudden and intrinsically successful, reversal of the presently downward-plunging economies of both the Americas and of western and central Europe. These would be, specifically, the principles of economy of the great American geniuses in economics such as Benjamin Franklin, General Alexander Hamilton, and such specific followers of Hamilton as the Presidents Abraham Lincoln, William McKinley, Franklin D. Roosevelt, and John F. Kennedy, but, also, including, actually useful, recent Presidents of good intentions and skills in their own persons, such as, recently, Republican Ronald Reagan and Democrat William Clinton (no Bushes included). Since then, there has been a worsening of the recently worse-than-useless Presidencies. The actual (i.e. net physical) economy of the United States, since the assassination of President John F. Kennedy, has been driven in a net downward trend-line motion, in fact, since the beginning of the 1970s.[10]

All of the habituated trends in U.S. policy-directions have been, overall, disasters not to be perpetuated; they have all been cardinal disasters for the United States, and, above all, for our population at large.

---

10. The recently notable exceptions have been, most notably, President Ronald Reagan (of SDI fame) and peacemaker President William Clinton.

Our National Intellectual Sickness

The downward trend of the physical economy, *per capita*, is to be measured, essentially, not in money, but presently accelerating degrees of collapse in physical economy, together with the deterioration of intellectual capabilities, and of the physical conditions of life and culture of the population generally. These have been, generally, downwards intellectually, and with respect to public health, with each succeeding new generation of predominantly incompetent, addictions-ridden adolescents and younger ages, alike, presently.

For example, the promotion of the spread of a mind-busting national drug-recreation-habit and, unfortunately, correlated intrinsically fraudulent cures, alike, has driven the present youthful and middle-aged population, down from the quality of a leading skilled work-force of the world, as in the time of President John F. Kennedy and Kennedy's most admirably productive contemporaries in our nation's leadership, into a relatively tiny minority portion of the post-adolescent and older, potentially useful work-force; but, worse, to a relatively incompetent, and pitiable unstable, relatively tiny fraction of the adult population as a whole. The fostering of the use of narcotic and related substances, and personal social practices designed for comparable effects, has produced the effect of a labor-force, chiefly without actually productive skills, or even a meager level of economic and social competence. The abundantly worse-than-useless, vastly excessively influential, and abominably super-wealthy, seem to present us with a weak-brained, ill-fed, utterly confused so-called "labor force," mainly without significant skills, and also rapidly vanishing options for continuing even mere subsistence, all the while the greatest Wall Street hyperinflation in all modern history, crushes the remaining mass of the population under the weight of the unpayable debt of those who are the merely financially rich, but the worst than useless for the needs of mankind presently.

A sweeping correction of those ills accumulated during and since the war which John F. Kennedy and General Douglas MacArthur had forbidden, is urgently needed, as an immediate reform, if our nation is to survive at all. In brief, Europe generally, and the Americas, too, have fallen into the same trap of evil, a cult of Zeus-

The worse-than-useless, vastly influential, and abominably super-wealthy, coexist alongside a weak-brained, ill-fed, utterly confused so-called "labor force," without significant skills, and rapidly vanishing options for continuing even mere subsistence.

Satan worship, exemplified presently by that quasi-global, British imperial monarchy, which has been modelled upon the proximate precedent of the, frankly, inherently Satanic Roman Empire.

The predators of trans-Atlantic region, are worse than useless speculators, sucking, intellectually and financially, on the proceeds of Wall Street and those related monetarist speculations, which have dominated and looted the economies of the trans-Atlantic economy, that done ever-more vividly, as a presently downward-accelerating trend, since the onset of the term of office of President Richard Nixon: the falsely, merely apparent (if only to the duped), net gains have always been merely nominal; the far more important, physical trends, have always been downward, if in more or less degree, during the passage of lapsed time since the close of the U.S.A.'s 1960s.

Why the U.S. Economy Has Plunged Downward

All progress by living processes, has been, and remains, premised upon the intrinsically needed rise in the interrelated sets of productive capabilities of mixed groups of living species, the human species, far above all. Progress on this account, is always expressed as in net effect, an upwardly evolutionary process of human cultural development into higher relative levels of per-capita energy-flux densities (as measurable in terms of reference to human chemistries/energy-flux densities of per capita, productive practice), excepting for exceptional, planetary catastrophes. The only exception to that requirement, is the human species, which increases its role among living species only voluntarily, rather than by simply biological interactions among species of plant, animal, etc., or, as by interactions among the set.

Only the human will is an exception to the rule, that all animal species otherwise, each, animal or vegetable, progress merely as a species, and that, implicitly only temporarily, except by a humanly determined influence on them: as V.I. Vernadsky has produced the evidence for this view of the relations respectively distinguishing the human species' upward self-evolution absolutely superior to both inferior living species, and to those human populations which resist their indispensably upward accelerating, physical-economical progress per-capita, upon which the continued existence of the human species itself, ultimately depends. This gain is a feature of the demonstration of the exceptional case of mankind: mankind as embodying the living processes of the uniquely human creative actions, which distinguish the human species, from all other living species otherwise known to us.

This power of the human will, depends upon a biologically evolutionary process, one which is integrally not only bio-chemical but willful. The specificity of the uniquely human property of the noëtic will is the ability and determination to continue to rise to ever higher developments achieved, in the fruitful realization of upward progress by means of ever-higher per-capita energy-flux densities of useful action, which is the most essential distinction of the human species' successful abilities, against all supposed animal alternative forms of life. Precisely that, is the most essential expression of the human will, known, essentially, as expressed, historically by the voluntary employment of the necessary use of fire as the "fuel" of the human species' willfully voluntary rise to ever higher orders of usefully expressed increases of the relative energy-flux density of the efficiently per-capita powers of the membership of the human species.

Man's Enemies: Zeus, Satan & the British Empire

The measure of that humanly voluntary increase of the energy-flux density of the human will, per capita and per unit of energy-flux density, is expressed in the notion of the famous *Promethean Principle*, as opposed to the currently "Green," Satanic-Zeusian principle embodied in both the myths of worship of the oligarchical pestilences known, interchangeably as the wicked systems of tyranny such as what has been known recently, as both the Roman and British empires.[11]

The presently clearest, and, also, exemplary, scientific account of the distinctions to be considered on this account, is located for chemistry by the physical development of a rate of increase of power of the human biologically, done through rises which correspond, in fair description for our purposes here: to the process of man's rising power of the role of chemistry, as measurable, in effect, in higher degrees of the power of the human species' unique option for the practicing of successively higher ranges of living chemistry.

For example: The Meaning of Modern Chemistry

Beginning with the Nineteenth-century process which had led into the Nineteenth Century's concluding decisions respecting the effects orderable in the mode which became known as physical chemistry, such as that of the famous Periodic Table. This occurred during the course of the Twentieth Century, when the "original Periodic Table" came to be recognized as an evolutionary process within the original framework of the Periodic Table, with the demonstrably evolutionary contributions to insight into a mankind-driven increase in the range of the so-called "elements" of the original conception of the periodic table as such, as shown by the study of the evolution into higher, synthetic powers of upward evolution, largely (for us presently) through elementarities beyond the original notions of radioactive chemistry: the higher energy-flux densities of the new chemistries produced within the range of the Twentieth Century and beyond, have been, and will be even far more advanced in adducible energy-flux ranges in densities of energy-flux densities, implicitly, at least potentially, than the indicated point-by-point potential of our Sun itself.

On this account, truly competent modern science, contrary to the pro-Satanic, "Green" dogma, has provided those who care, with appropriate insights into the

---

11. I.e., the "oligarchical principle" of the Zeus-Satan cultural formations. Rather than, for example, the Christian Apostolic Principle, which was always intrinsically Promethean when properly informed as to effect and intention: a dedication to the future mission of mankind's development through the uniquely noëtic powers specific to the human species, against the intrinsically Satanic, "green" ideologies.

'Original' Periodic Table of Elements

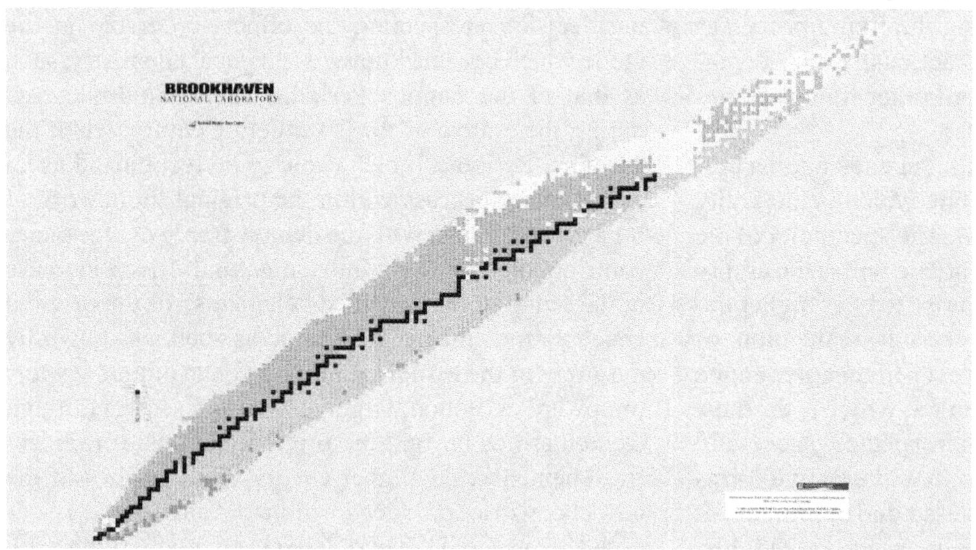

FIGURE 2
'New' Periodic Table: Nuclides

implications of the work of the greatest modern exponent of human life as such, in the implications of the achievements of the most important modern scientist of life this far, V.I. Vernadsky. Today, the fact is, that mankind has achieved the demonstrable design, as this had been done by mankind ourselves, which reaches beyond the range of the energy-flux density of the expressed power of energy-flux densities, if only in detail, higher than those of the Sun as a whole, presently. That signifies, that mankind's present potential has reached, already, experimentally, inherently energy-flux densities beyond any otherwise presently known means within the known bounds of Johannes Kepler's uniquely effective discovery of the principled existence of the Solar system as such.

The consequent fact is, that the noëtic powers of the human mind will almost certainly come to exceed (implicitly) those known abilities of the Sun which are implicitly inferior to the implicitly promised, higher order of constructs and products of the practice of the human mind.

Mind: thus now signifies, that the powers of the human mind's continued, upward development in power of practice, pertain to an inherent characteristic of the human mind, as such, rather than the mere functions of the human brain as such. This distinction, which lies beyond the reach of all presently known experiences of mere human sense-perception, reflects a kind of power which excludes any merely animal life *per se*. It is a power which reaches far beyond the powers of human sense-perception, such that only man's progressively advancing process of creation of this effect, enables mankind to efficiently recognize those powers in the universe whose distinction is, that they exceed, implicitly, and also entirely, the bounds of relatively miserable, original human experiences of mere sense-perception.

On that just-stated account, the particular case of the work of Vladimir I. Vernadsky, time itself is inferior to the specific talent of human creativity. This was the emphasis which he had reached in the course of the evidence of his work: man, thus, must create himself, upwardly going, in a direction of developments intending to seek endlessly ultimate relative perfection in the goals of human creative progress itself within that Solar space originally discovered by Johannes Kepler, and beyond. Thus, merely biology, as it had been customarily defined even among most merely technical scientists of our present time, had been a power qualitatively inferior to the characteristics specific to the actual potentials of the human mind, as the great scientists arisen from the Nineteenth and Twentieth centuries had done. Science in its right name and true nature, exists only beyond the wretched limits of merely human sense-perception: it lies in the effects which are to be recognized as beyond the reach of merely sense-perception as such, and beyond "whoever might have gone before us."

So, in such a circumstance, Eratosthenes' discovery of the magnitude of the Earth, was a relatively early kind of a masterful type of true knowledge, reaching beyond the meager means of mere human sense-perception, as a true science, gained from the observation of the true object of the image which the Sun of the Solar system casts upon Earth. It was an image, to be seen in the mirror defined for this purpose, as the footprint of the Sun which represents a truth beyond the pitiably silly presumptions of merely human sense-perception *per se*.

With that measure, which had reached to levels far superior to Archimedes's merely reductionist's abilities, mankind, is actually knowledgeable in a quality and degree, far beyond the reach of mere sense-perception: the principle of knowledge, had always departed the illusion of mere human sense-perception, into coming to actually know the Earth as far beyond the mere human personal sense-perception. Mankind continues to view the events on Earth as ontologically from far above mere sense-perception, as such. This must be done, now, from the minimax principle of Johannes Kepler's discovery of the Solar system, into the Galaxy and states of entities far above that, wherein the ever new truths about man, are now waiting to be discovered.

Such is the basis for the continuing development of mankind's knowledge of science into regions of knowledge far superior to mere human sense-perception as such: beyond all of the silly notions of mere sense-certainty *per se*.

Such, immediately above here, leads our attention into the more urgent considerations which I will now outline for you, below, as follows:

II. The Crucial Role of V.I. Vernadsky

In the meantime, during the still-living achievements of Russia's Vladimir Ivanovich Vernadsky,[12] the greatest scientific discoveries of universal principle have, so far, only been touched, while being, already, presently, the most crucial knowledge of physical science yet to be discovered: knowledge which relatively immediately, awaits us, but still unattended by most of even the seemingly best-informed human scientific minds.

In brief, V.I. Vernadsky was the original discoverer of the most important principle presently available to only the very best among modern physical science. There is no proper justification for tolerating the all-too prevalent, backward view of the current state of science-topical affairs. The subject which I now introduce immediately, does have, conveniently, certain characteristic appearances of a preliminary nature, which are qualified to prompt preliminary insights into the territory on which I am reporting here.

On this specific account, it would be incompetence, for me to neglect taking into account my own knowledge respecting the distinction between the Soviet Union as a reflection of the scientific and artistic culture of Russia prior to the Bolshevik Revolution, and the complexities inherent in the evolutionary social process of the Soviet Union's infiltration by, chiefly elements recruited, such as the British dupe, A.I. Oparin, into the process, by the corruption of British intelligence operations linked to the inherently Satanic Bertrand Russell, as that is now to be considered with respect to the conditions since the influence of the initially British establishment of the installation of the Adolf Hitler regime. Consider this matter, in the following terms:

The Franklin D. Roosevelt Factor Cuts In

It is commonly said among decent people, that President Franklin D. Roosevelt was a true genius, whose passion had done wonders, the like of which, no other person of the Twentieth Century had matched. Indeed, much of the "secret" of President Franklin Roosevelt's works of true genius, was manifest only after his recovery-inspired inspiration, as expressed as his miraculous upward surge of his intellectual creativity had, itself,

12. Aka: V.I. Vernadsky.

lived long enough to inspire, also, such as the John F. Kennedy inspired by widow Eleanor Roosevelt, and John's own brother, Robert. V.I. Vernadsky would have implicitly agreed with such an outlook, and that is not merely as an adornment.

Such considerations engage a profound principle of our universe (at least for as much as scientists generally know as both the Solar system and defeating the hazards of the journeys through the tracks of the Galaxy which contains it). V.I. Vernadsky's virtually miraculous mind, touches upon such higher ranges of matters located within particularly important celestial processes. Such is the human mind's potential, which actually dwells within that domain, which we are, currently, usually left more to admire than to manage; but, notwithstanding all commonplaces, V.I. Vernadsky has been the greatest well-known scientist in respect to his actually accomplished and still living achievements, this far. If you think differently, it is clear than you must have missed the most important, presently knowable, scientific facts.

This is not merely justified praise of his accomplishments; there is a much more profound issue to be considered, and that very seriously, all for pressing practical reasons, on this account.

Against the background of the immediately preceding paragraphs, above, there is a second general observation, which complements a related, also crucially important, subject matter, a matter on which V.I. Vernadsky's fundamental discoveries in physical science, live in the very foundations of the actual meaning of the human mind. I identify that point as a first consideration, as a key point for this part of the report.

Summarily: the central achievement of the great scientist called Vladimir Ivanovich Vernadsky's principles of universal scientific practice, can be located in his demand for the discarding of the claims to the meager existence of the notion of an independent prin-

"V.I. Vernadsky's fundamental discoveries in physical science live in the very foundations of the actual meaning of the human mind."

ciple of *time per se*. The creative powers of mankind, rather than time as such, are the essential metric of mankind's achievement of knowledge of the universe: the truly fundamental scientific principle of practice is that of the actual "clock to be kept," the imagined clock of the ontologically willfully anti-entropic progress of the human species, as opposed to belief in objects floating within the opinions of those less articulate scientists who define themselves, foolishly, as being located within a merely imagined physical space and time. In fact, the most essential parameters, so employed, are, relatively speaking, one very big "boo-boo," that of overlooking of essential and otherwise well known, factual evidence: there is much too much reliance on the intellectual quicksands of belief in mere sense-perception *per se*.

Consider the merely apparent controversy which my own immediate remarks here might, mistakenly, presume, as if, out of the scientific ignorance expressed as believing in a physical space-time premised upon a merely notional principle of the functions of merely *space-time matter.* They may admire the idea of science, as that may be properly said: but, actually, they have the principles of that which are only ostensibly scientific: which is to say belief in reality "bass-ackwards." Rather, as V.I. Vernadsky stated his point with both the utmost clarity and scientific truth, as well: it is mankind's own existence, as V.I. Vernadsky also argues, which actually measures the superior, if seemingly only some more powerful shadow-like attributes of mankind's actually determining existence of a really living, uniquely human species: as a force within not only the future history of mankind, but a reflection of the true law of the universe, from the top, down, not the bottom-up.

Man may be imperfectly educated, if otherwise skilled; but, the imperfectly practicing professional scientists, tend toward what should be an obviously mistaken presumption of their belief in falsely premised, essentially crucial omissions of regard for the essentially inclusive, most crucial, actually experimental facts in available evidence. There are several crucial, higher categories involved: which we must take into account as interlocking categories of the systemically erroneous, but also commonplace, ontological presumptions.

The essential blunder, which even almost every scientifically respectable professional, usually, makes, up to recently known date, is the plausible, but, more correctly named also stupid presumption, that mankind's existence is, *a-priori*: which is to claim that man is situated within the context of the mere reductionist's silly notion of physical space-time. Admittedly, the false presumption, in other words, is the presumption that life, as such, is, itself, a product of the reductionist's imagined notion of an axiomatically, mathematical-physical space-time: a belief, or merely a set of presumptions, which is to be counted, essentially, as just another kind of example of the malicious idiocies of the Twentieth Century's foolish David Hilbert, and, of the relatively contemporary, and frankly Satanic, Bertrand Russell, and the latter's like.[13]

The origin of the commonplace fallacy which I treat here, is best attributed to the adoption of a certain blinded faith, to the effect, of an axiomatic presumption of the essentially mythical blind faith in a presumed functional quality of "elementarity" attributed to human sense-perception *per se: a delusion which had been already discredited by the importantly discovered principle of Eratosthenes' measurement of the Earth. It is the delusion of belief in a sense-perceptual phenomenon of human sense-perception, as lying within the domain of sense-perception of an object within the atmosphere of Earth, as compared to the* transit of the cycle of the observation of the position of the Sun lying outside the imagined atmosphere of human sense-perception.

It is, as a matter of principle, that, the experience of the humanly attributed rotation and displacement of the relative position of the Sun, were an ironical matter, respecting an irony essentially unknown until the triad of the combined notions of the minimum principle of Filippo Brunelleschi, the maximum of Nicholas of Cusa (without elementary linear characteristics) and the third, essential part of the essential conception: the principle expressed in Johannes Kepler's discovery of the inherent principle of motion within the identity of the Solar system, which exists only without, rather than merely within.

This is to be compared with the viciously reductionist error inherent in the presumptions of the otherwise very clever and energetic Archimedes. It is, ultimately, the universe itself, which is actually elementary as a process: just as life *per se* can not be the product of a reductionist phenomenon. In fact, it is a true universal principle of the universe, that the particular phenomenon can only be a fruit of the relatively encompassing universality, as Carl F. Gauss carefully avoided telling what he had known in the circumstances posed (indirectly to him) by young Bolyai, and the latter's own father.[14] The time was not ripe for him to say certain things he knew very well; he had wisely, and certainly implicitly, trusted the future accomplishments of his brilliant protégé, Bernhard Riemann, then, on the occasion, presenting a great work, Riemann's historic Habilitation Dissertation, presented in the honoring of his great mentor, Carl F. Gauss.

Discussion:

What had struck my attention, on this account, had been, that since the British empire had used the death of President Franklin D. Roosevelt as the opportunity to continue World War II under a commitment to a nuclear conflict with the Soviet Union, and a reign of terror inside the U.S.A. itself, all under the virtually terrorist reign of the foolish Harry S Truman: which had left the Soviet Union itself with an internal division of notability, between those who adhered to their connections with the British Empire, as Bertrand Russell's worse-than-Nazi trained, intellectual dupe, the typical reductionist of Russell pedigree, such as A.I. Oparin, versus the actually scientific cultural outlook of V.I. Vernadsky, who has been, since his death in 1945, a crucial, available instrument of modern science for the foster-

---

13. This is, by no means, even a slight exaggeration. It is largely a folly to be blamed on the conditioning of students in their classrooms, or related circumstances, which prompts them to rely on taught-down teachings of the classrooms and related circumstances. Their teachers, textbooks, classrooms, popular opinions, and so on have taught them down into swallowing it, as prevalently acceptable presumptions in the mode of commonplace matters of mere opinion, whether gained from passing quips of the classroom, or similarly reckless modes of defining of so-called, merely popular opinion.

14. See: C.F. Gauss to F. Bolyai, from Göttingen: June 3, 1832: the work of the great mind of Gauss himself, presented to ease the tension expressed by Farkas Bolyai, the father, respecting the subject presented by the son, Janos Bolyai. Carl Friedrich Gauss: **"Der Fürst der Mathematikers" in Briefen und Gesprächen.** Kurt R. Biermann, Verlag C.H. Beck, Munich, 1990. An interesting posture by Gauss, in dealing with the passions of the father and son respecting the inherent evil of Euclidean geometry.

ing of the rescue of the world from the nightmares which the British Empire's Bertrand Russell had foisted as an evil, upon a post-President Franklin Roosevelt's heritage, up through the times of a number of the presently ongoing, Federal incumbencies since the administration of President Franklin Roosevelt, in particular.

The crucial fact, respecting U.S. laws' insolent evasions of the U.S. Federal Constitution, has been the increasing rate of a general lack of actual principle, by the great majority of former Presidents of the United States: a majority which had made way for the production of particular laws which were, then, and are, now, inherently violations of the underlying intention of principle for the Federal Constitution. Treasury Secretary Alexander Hamilton was assassinated, by the British Empire's agent, Aaron Burr, to protect the corruption of the U.S. Constitution, in the name of "States Rights," the "States Rights" fraud against the U.S. Constitution, supported by some Presidents such as, early on, John Adams, Thomas Jefferson, and James Madison. U.S. Presidents Monroe and John Quincy Adams, had restored the United States to its Constitutional intention, in repudiating the errors of Adams, Jefferson, and Madison.

The professional British assassin, Aaron Burr had financed the British imposition of the introduction of the British interest against the United States, executed by the criminal figures of Andrew Jackson and Martin Van Buren; and, there was no effective President from that time, until the President Abraham Lincoln, whose leadership had saved the United States.

Naturally the British empire, personally, had organized, from operations launched in Canada, the assassination of President Abraham Lincoln and other British targets in the U.S. during the same time.

These historical facts, respecting the United States' government and its history, bear essentially on nations such as Russia today, still, because the United States, which had been created to serve as an instrument for spreading human freedom throughout the world, had been so often turned by the British empire and its Wall Street money-maker elements, into either a simply powerless U.S. national leadership, or an utterly corrupted one, by the influence of the British imperial interests globally. Vernadsky's contributions to all humanity's benefit, were in the process of being realized through the role of President Franklin Roosevelt, during the relevant moment of world history; the death of that President followed, who would have, otherwise, saved the planet from the prospect of new world wars, which

has ensued since, through the British Empire's control over the U.S. Government, through the accession of the inherently disgusting, puppet of Winston Churchill, and, more significantly, the truly Satanic figure of pure evil, world-war-maker and mass murderer otherwise, Bertrand Russell.

Consider thus, the submission of Presidents to the powers of the British agents known collectively as Wall Street; the root of these evils has been the lack of an actual notion of physical principle, a deficiency which was made way for, by the British-like substitution of merely current shifts in proximate opinion as an unprincipled notion of matters bearing on Constitutional law: beginning with the case of the intentional fraud against the Federal Constitution known as "States Rights," and the international implications of using a "States Rights" basis, as was done in the State of Virginia, against the actual intention of the Federal Constitution, as was done by such Presidents as John Adams, Thomas Jefferson, and James Madison: the "loophole in the Federal Constitution" through which herds of British elephants might have marched (and often did) without effective obstruction: a mere confederation of states, intentionally circumventing the Federal Constitution, as Adams, Jefferson, and Madison, had done, as had Jefferson in abandoning his office under President George Washington—while professional British assassins such as Aaron Burr could have created the evil, openly and explicitly, which would become the skunks Andrew Jackson and Martin Van Buren. Profiting against the United States, is a practice which leans toward treason against the most precious principles of our Republic.[15]

The very meaning of United States of America, under the design of its Federal Constitution, had been that the states are subjects of the Constitution of the

---

15. Notably, money as such has no honorable principle. It is merely a means of exchange, honorable only as a charge against the sovereign nation-state which has uttered its currency; that is key for understanding what has corrupted our United States' Government increasingly, as with the inherent corruption of substituting money-as-such for the same physical principles of progress which inhere in the practices, respecting the use of money, by the four fundamental rules of Treasury Secretary Alexander Hamilton, on which the foundations of the economy of the republic of the United States had depended. Anything contrary to that principle, is and would be a fraud against the principle on which the United States was created. All true economic value is intrinsically physical, not monetary, as Treasury Secretary Alexander Hamilton had defined the relevant notion of national currency used as a means for exchange, within the nation, or, in other currencies, by other nations, for physical goods in fact.

"The metric of evolution in the Solar System itself, is not merely life-forms, but, only, as known this far, the self-evolution of the human will unique to the human species' own principle of a universal chemistry, the increase of the energy-flux density enabling the progressive evolution upward of mankind itself...." Shown: the center of the Milky Way Galaxy.

United States, and are obliged to conduct their foreign trade accordingly. Hamilton's assassination, as the greatest economist of the original United States, since the death of Benjamin Franklin, has been, as Treasurer, and also a Major-General, the leading representative of the design for the U.S. economy, who had created the world's greatest economic-policy design in world history so far, was assassinated by the British imperial interest. The great evil to be destroyed, on this account, still today, is the failure to recognize that the mere money of any actually sovereign nation has no intrinsic value, other than the trade in physical values within itself, or in uniquely physically actual traffic among others.[16] Only such precautions can assure the actual sovereignty of any individual national republic, if it expresses, more or less perfectly, its truly efficient sovereignty, free from submission to foreign powers and their agencies. In short, Wall Street, and its like, must neatly and summarily, be put out of existence, for reason of the continuing, systemic existential fraud.[17]

The relevant implication for that argument by me in this present report, is that the wisdom of nations, in practice, can only be expressed globally in one of two ways: either agreements in human economic policies echoing the original American settlements on behalf of freedom for all peoples, but, that including such essentially historical predecessors as the great Renaissance's Brunelleschi, Cardinal Nicholas of Cusa, and their essential representative Johannes Kepler, with his unique discovery of the Solar system and its underlying scientific principle. However, the contemporary realization of that intention depends presently, upon a very specific role of the greatest scientist, in effect, who has been, so far, V.I. Vernadsky's discovery of the living meaning of the human species in both past, and present universal history.

The Very Crucial Implications: The Options

The crucial importance of Russia at this moment, lies in the implications of the continuation of the relatively unique scientific legacy of V.I. Vernadsky, for both Russians and large sectors from among the Ukrainians: the true, presently living spirit of national unity of elements of Russo-Ukrainian culture when considered in its history as representing a basis for a Eurasian unity in economic and related practice. The best hope for the planet as a whole, at this juncture, will be, virtually uniquely, a Eurasian alliance of its own, most able, and best with the United States itself. Only consider the implications of the wonderful potential of emphasis on leaps forward in thermonuclear fusion's role in increasing the level of applied energy-flux density to a mankind, still on our planet, but reaching out from Earth to bring a needed, humanly directed development into,

---

16. E.g., value under the standard of V.I. Vernadsky's principle of intrinsically human value.

17. This means, as I have stressed earlier, that there must be a transformation of the U.S. national banking system, conducted under the authority of the Secretary of the Treasury, which bans all banking, except-

ing national banking, by national executive authority of the Treasury *per se*. Federal decrees and related decisions under Federal regulation are to be applied accordingly.

initially nearby regions of Solar space, through robotic systems controlled from Earth, but, nonetheless gaining a power within the Solar system itself, which are a source of the power needed to maintain the Sun as viable factor in the protection and development of the Solar system, and of the challenges which accelerated leaps higher, scientifically, within the Solar system, will make feasible for our humble living-space back here, on Earth. For example: NASA restored and amplified for its role as an increasingly potent and effective planetary factor within, and ultimately beyond the mere Solar system itself.

With the termination of institutions such as the pro-Satanic cases of the Roman Empire and the present British empire, the historically imperialist systems of ancient and present times, must vanish from the practices of the planet, immediately. The careers of the likes of the Zeus and Satan, such as the Roman and British empires, must be brought to submission to a cooperative order among the sovereign republics, who must now triumph over the, actually pro-Satanic, oligarchicalist imperial tradition, such as the present British Empire. Let the nations choose their independent identities, as President Franklin D. Roosevelt had intended for as long as he had remained alive: the means by which the progressive future of mankind, throughout, and beyond this planet, must now prosper.

However, there are certain particular considerations which must be actively brought into play, to enable the realization of such goals as I have specified, heretofore, in a competent vision of the present and future times, as now follows, here, immediately, next.

Vernadsky's Unique Principle of Mankind

As I had indicated, in this present report, earlier, the realization of the goals which I have identified here, this far, depends upon an urgent need for systemic revision of the heretofore present notion of the specific practical role of mankind within the Solar system itself, as such. That is to emphasize, that the heretofore accepted notions of mankind's efficient place within both the Solar systemic system, and beyond, must be radically rectified, and that strictly according to the particular standard stipulated by V.I. Vernadsky. Mankind must now be recognized as the supreme power operating within the process of development of mankind's policies of practice respecting relations within and of the Solar system as a whole: that as Vernadsky had strictly emphasized while he had been still living.

We must now recognize, that space and time no longer exist of themselves as reliable notions, nor with actually practical efficiency for mankind; only the role assigned to mankind by our given nature, has useful merit, precisely as V.I. Vernadsky has made that point. Mankind itself, is the only proper determinant of the practical meaning of what is, mistakenly called a basis based upon a mistaken notion of an actual combination of time, space, and matter, presently popularly presumed to be available to humanity's will. The actual basis is only the creative (i.e., noëtic) powers attributable to the individual human mind, expressed through increase of the power of the human species to change the course of development of the life of the human species within (immediately) the Solar system as such: Vernadsky's most essential expression of the identifiably essential principle of the existence of our human species.

A Universal Principle:

The metric of evolution in the Solar system itself, is not merely life-forms-in-general; but, only, as known this far, the self-evolution of the human will unique to the human species' own principle of a universal chemistry, the principled increase of the energy-flux density enabling the progressive evolution upward of mankind itself: the evolution of mankind which prompts the increased power expressed as higher characteristic evolutions upward by the societies of the human species, into constant rises in the power of mankind's self-existence and effective revolutionary progresses in mankind's appropriate authority for the evolution of the Solar systemic system as a whole, immediately. My words, in my time, but his (Vernadsky's) explicitly stated intention.

By wielding the upward evolution of both the preconditions and evolutions of the effective power, per capita, in coordination with a rise in the living human progress to higher potencies of energy-flux densities through the means of what we name as upward-evolving chemistry as mankind's characteristic abilities, mankind daily resets the clock of the Solar system's future, as done through the means and requirements for great leaps in the applicable energy-flux density of each nation, each people, and each willing person, whose effective role must be leaps in the power of mankind within the universe, *per capita*. That is the expression of true human nature to be known: which reflects the leading revolutionary achievements of the magnificent poet of human reason, the late V.I. Vernadsky, and of principled scientific will.